JAMES WARDELL

Canadian Cataloguing in Publication Data

Kirk, Janis Foord, 1948 —
    Surviving the upheaval in your workplace

(A Career monitor series)
ISBN 0-9695936-0-0

1. Vocation guidance. 2. Job hunting.
3. Career development. 4. Work environment.
I. Title. II. Series

HF5382.5.C2K57 1992   331.25   C92-094012-9

**Neither the publisher nor the author is rendering legal or
other professional advice in this book. If such assistance is
required, the services of a competent professional should
be sought.**

ACKNOWLEDGEMENTS

When a book builds over weeks and months as this one has, it develops a life of its own. *Career Monitor* first appeared in the Toronto Star business pages on October 20, 1990. Though the job market was tight back then and had been for some time, few people had uttered the dreaded R word — recession. Yet within months, it became so commonplace in our vocabulary we hardly noticed it. And all around us, the workplace began to change.

Over the many difficult months that followed, our financial problems deepened and the pace of change accelerated. The upheaval has been tremendous. Even as the economy recovers, most analysts predict the rapid rate of change will continue.

Many of the people featured in these collected columns have been casualties of this upheaval, others have been observers whose comments have helped the rest of us relate their experiences to the broader social context. Interwoven throughout are the thoughts of caring professionals in my field who so willing passed on their wisdom and advice. Their stories, comments and suggestions have chronicled this chaotic time. I'd like to thank them all.

Thank you, as well, to The Star's Saturday editor, Dennis Morgan, and to the entire Business Today staff. A special thanks to Kim Sherman, who so efficiently and sensitively handles readers' calls and letters each week.

To my supportive colleagues at Murray Axmith and Associates, the outplacement firm where I hang my hat several days each week, my gratitude for the professional sounding board you all provide when I need to discuss difficult issues or gain a fresh perspective.

The cover, design and polish of this book are the handiwork of Shelley and Peter Robertson of Inprint Editorial Services, who worked tirelessly to make it the special publication it is. Thank you both for your commitment to excellence, which never fails to inspire me.

And to David, my husband, best friend, partner and editor, my deepest, heartfelt thanks. Without you, without your support, this book wouldn't exist.

CONTENTS

FOREWORD

March 5, 1992
Toronto

"Upheaval."

The word speaks volumes. In my 18 years in career redirection, I have never experienced such a potent combination of stress, uncertainty and change as the wave of restructuring currently sweeping the business world. On every side, the workplace is undergoing a profound transformation, and survival is on just about everybody's mind.

What's more, this state of affairs is not confined to Canada. It is global. Everywhere I go these days, every time I visit one of our offices, I hear the same theme. The old ways of doing business are no longer adequate. Times are changing, and organizations of all kinds have to change with them.

To the workers called upon to change as well, this presents a kind of Catch 22. They may recognize the imperative, but they can't yet see what lies ahead, or how to manage the transition.

In many different and important ways, career professionals are doing their best to help.

Janis Foord Kirk is one of them. The message in these collected columns is a message of hope, founded on careful self-evaluation and basic human values. It comes not only from her, but from the people she counsels and the readers who write to her, all of them struggling to keep their careers on course in uncertain times.

It's a valuable book, not because it offers some miraculous solution (there isn't one) but because it directs itself to the individual and the individual's problems. And that, I feel strongly, is the fundamental key to surviving these difficult times.

Corporations, governments and labor unions share enormous responsibility as circumstances continue to evolve. Training, as the book points out, is an indispensable part of the picture. The resources needed to upgrade skills are rarely within the grasp of the ordinary worker.

But ultimately, tens, even hundreds of thousands of individuals will have to find solutions that work — for them. The cumulative effect of their best efforts will provide the successful transition we seek for the workplace as a whole.

Murray Axmith

Chapter 1

ADVERSITY...
AND WHAT
YOU MAKE OF IT

ALFRED WONG

For a good many people, the '90s are proving to be trying times, fraught with more problems than any of us can remember. Try as we might to get a clear sense of the future, we can't. Uncertainty and change are the order of the day.

The uncertainty is the most trying. Our country's political problems have been plaguing us for too long. The national economy is unpredictable; the international climate volatile at best.

Equally troubling is the employment scene. And its troubles are unlikely to disappear, as the decade unfolds and the labor market continues to shift and rumble beneath us.

People at all levels of the workforce, those looking for jobs as well as those trying to manage the ones they have, are caught in a multiple dilemma — shrinking wages and obsolescent industries, superimposed on the unprecedented challenge of a rapidly globalizing market.

> Attitude plays a key role in determining whether you're challenged or overwhelmed.

This combination means that straightforward, predictable career growth is no longer possible. Increasingly, people are confronted with the need to develop new skills or upgrade the ones they've got.

However complicated things get, it's important to recognize that you, as an individual, still have some power, some control. Your attitude can affect your situation positively or negatively; it's fundamentally important, playing a key role in determining whether you're challenged by times like these or overwhelmed.

These are not the first rough times. Nor are we the first to face them. It's helpful to remember other times and other people and to remind ourselves of the qualities that helped them survive and eventually flourish anew.

One talented young man who had — in abundance — the ability to pick himself up, dust off, learn from his misfortunes and carry on, began his career in Kansas City in the early 1920s.

He started out full of enthusiasm, and put everything he had into a business venture. Despite some modest success, within a couple of years his company, which made animated films, went bankrupt.

"It was probably the blackest time of my life," he is quoted as saying. "I really knew what hardship and hunger was like.... It was a pretty lonely and miserable time of my life."

Still, this was an enterprising fellow who talked his creditors into letting him keep his camera. He got freelance photography work, and soon paid off his personal debts. He bought a first-class train ticket to California.

Within a few years, he was in business again. This venture became a huge success. Today, the man, Walt Disney, and his creation, Mickey Mouse, are known throughout the world.

With a little investigation, you'd find the determination that moulded Walt Disney's career in the bag of tricks successful people in many fields use to build their own careers. Throughout history, people have often turned adverse circumstances around by simply refusing to give up.

As another case in point, look at this curriculum vitae of a U.S. politician from the 1800s.

> Failed in business ('31)
> Defeated for Legislature ('32)
> Again, failed in business ('33)
> Elected to Legislature ('34)
> Sweetheart died ('36)
> Had nervous breakdown ('36)
> Defeated for Speaker ('38)
> Defeated for Senate ('40)
> Married ('42)
> Elected to Congress ('46)
> Son died ('50)
> Defeated for Senate ('55)
> Defeated for vice-president ('56)
> Defeated for Senate ('58)
> Elected President ('60)

The man was Abraham Lincoln, who during his presidency changed the course of North American history.

People can be enormously resilient. Their ambitions are not always as lofty as those of the legendary Lincoln, but their abilities to bounce back, to struggle through adversity and emerge the better for it, are frequently as inspirational.

The columns collected here offer suggestions on ways to go about looking for work. More important, perhaps, they look at how ordinary people cope, or try to, in tough times. The stories are diverse, sometimes uplifting, occasionally discouraging. But more often than not, they reveal the tremendous creativity that flows out of the need to survive, and the fundamental importance of a positive attitude.

These are not easy times to make decisions about work. In many ways, though, they're the best possible times to learn about career planning. As we all learn to make our way through the challenges of the moment, imagine how much better prepared we'll be as new opportunities appear.

If you're out of work and trying to remain strong in the face of apprehension and anxiety, work hard to maintain your sense of self-worth.

Opportunities do exist in the job market, and key to finding them is attitude. Prepare well. Get your resume updated. Start into your network of contacts.

Spend time with people who make you feel good about yourself. And use this book to remind yourself of approaches and attitudes that have worked for others.

Above all, don't let your sense of your own value evaporate. These words from the 17th-century poet John Dryden put it well:

> *"I'm a little wounded,*
> *but I am not slain;*
> *I will lay me down and bleed for a while,*
> *then I'll rise and fight again."*

Chapter 2

CHANGE
IS HERE
TO STAY

JAMES WARDELL

"I magine. After that many years with a company, to be walked to the door at 3:30 in the afternoon by a guy you worked with and told you're no longer employed. It's pretty callous stuff."

That's how Peter J. describes losing his job. Even though he knew he was perceived as someone not in step with the organization, it still came as a shock. He's not completely over it yet. "Subconsciously and psychologically, it will always be there," Peter believes. "It will take a long time to go away."

Look closely behind stories like this and you'll always find complicated details — personality clashes, communication problems, differences in style.

Still, despite the complexities of his own situation, in many ways it was change that did Peter in. His company's priorities changed. His workplace changed. Management in his department changed. Times changed.

> "I like to think I changed with the times...
> but I guess I no longer fit their pattern."

"I like to think I changed along with them," Peter says. "I went back to school and got a degree, for instance. But I guess I no longer fit their pattern.

"And, politically, I made a lot of mistakes," he acknowledges. "So, I had no protection. I don't think it would've happened if I'd had protection."

While there might be some way to protect yourself from personality and style conflicts, it's unlikely Peter, or any of us, can protect ourselves from the changes revolutionizing our workplace. We are living in a time of immense upheaval.

All around us, the big arena in which all careers are played out is changing. Individuals and companies hoping to prosper in the years ahead will have to learn how to change along with it.

Recessionary times are not the cause of this change, although they do tend to increase the pitch and turn up the volume. In fact, our economic troubles have become something of a blind, masking other fundamental influences bubbling away beneath the surface.

Not only is the workplace changing, workers are changing as well — demographically speaking.

Experts have been warning it would happen for more than 20 years. The "smoke stack" industries will shrink and create fewer and fewer jobs, we were told. Employment growth would be in the service and information industries. The point has finally been made — graphically — by traumatic, first-hand experience.

These statistics from the *Royal Bank Reporter* substantiate it further:

- In 1970, just over 22 per cent of Canadian workers were employed in manufacturing; by 1990, that sector had shrunk to less than 16 per cent.
- Twenty years ago, only 26 per cent of the workforce worked in community, business and personal services; by 1990, that had increased to nearly 35 per cent.

And across North America, millions of jobs — some say up to 4 million — have disappeared since the '90s began.

Change of this magnitude constitutes a major restructuring, and Peter J. is just one of hundreds of thousands of casualties. The effects of the restructuring are further compounded by problems in the greater economy, and the result is uncertainty, even for those who have jobs. The questions are repeated again and again. What will this mean to our standard of living? To my job? To the future? To my children's future?

Particularly worrisome is that no one seems able to answer these questions. We're all learning and adapting as we go, just like Peter J.

And this means learning to manage change, says psychologist Marti Smye, president of the Toronto-based change management firm People Tech Consulting Inc.

The catalysts of change in the workplace are "the ones we read about all the time," says Smye, "globalization, de-regulation, the environment." Globalization is a major force, she says, and we're feeling it acutely because of our free trade pact with the U.S.

Organizations react to the demands of today's marketplace by developing different "organizational strategies," says Smye. They merge, or acquire another company, they restructure, they downsize (or, "rightsize," as it's sometimes called). "Whenever there's a new strategy, new vision, new CEO or new technology, the corporate culture changes," Smye says.

Sometimes this change evolves slowly, as it did in Peter J.'s case. More than a decade ago, his employer, a manufacturing company in the communications industry, decided to move into high-tech manufacturing and to penetrate international markets. A new president was hired, advanced technology was developed, management philosophy changed. The changes had been under way for years before Peter got tripped up.

More and more, however, the reverse is the norm. Change in the workplace is often thrust upon people suddenly, though rumors abound months before the actual announcement is made.

And when the corporate rumor mill is active, uncertainty is the by-product. Everyone knows something is percolating behind the scenes, but little concrete news filters down to middle managers and workers. Confusion reigns. The announcement, by the time it's finally made, only adds to the volatility.

What happens, says Smye, is that as an organization's priorities change, so do its expectations. People are simply expected to adapt. It's as if the company says: "Now we need people to behave differently."

Without doubt this will be the big challenge of the '90s, both for those who are employed and those in the job market. We'll all have to learn how to manage change and, somehow, to turn it to our advantage.

We are up to the challenge, though it requires a radically different perspective on the part of the individual and society at large. Many of our old perceptions are no longer valid.

> We need governments at all levels to take a more active supporting role through this very difficult transition.

"We have to shift our thinking to the sources of growth and wealth in the future," according to Laurent Thibault, co-chair of the National Workforce Development Board.

"We have to believe more strongly in the fact that the real strength of our country is going to be in the skills and knowledge base of its labor force," he says.

The labor force — that's us. You and me and Peter J. More than wheat, or minerals, or even forest products, the future growth and wealth of Canada depend on the skills we bring to the workforce.

But what skills?

How will we know? Whose job is it to help us find out?

Training and re-training of workers will "require the united efforts of governments, businesses and schools," says the *Royal Bank Reporter*.

Co-operation, in other words, will be required to a degree rarely — if ever — seen in the past.

We need governments at all levels to take a more active supporting role through this very difficult transition. We need educational institutions to work closely with both governments and corporations. In offices and on plant floors across the country, we need corporations to accept more responsibility, by preparing their workers and managers for change.

In short, we need enlightened leadership from people who can communicate exactly what it is workers are supposed to do differently in this new era.

To date, in the corporate world at least, "that seldom happens," says Marti Smye.

"CEOs develop a clear vision, a very clear view why they need to change the structure. But they never complete the vision," she contends. "They don't 'operationalize' it so people can understand what it means, what the change is going to look like, what a successful manager and a successful staff person is going to look like, what they will have to do differently."

Which means, for the moment at any rate, the onus is back on us. When it comes to coping with changes in the workplace, you and I and Peter J. are on our own.

If your organization is restructuring, Smye offers these suggestions to help you adapt:

Set goals.

"Go about your business," she advises. "Most people get scared. It's like the deer in the headlights — they freeze. Take action. You'll accomplish a lot more. You'll be moving ahead."

Take the initiative.

"If you see a need or an opening, reach out and take the initiative. You'll be perceived as being action-oriented. Initiative is always respected when any new culture is developing."

Stay off the gossip treadmill.

"If you have a complaint, take it to someone who can do something about it," she advises.

Talk to as many people as you can.

"Ask questions. Don't be aggressive, but try to get people to articulate just what the new rules are. Ask: 'How would you like us to be different? How does this apply to my job? How does my job fit into this new arena? What do you think I need to learn?'"

Keep an open mind.

"People are seen as not fitting because they're seen as resisting, not being able to try, not willing to make the shift. You don't have to lose your integrity," Smye says. "But before you decide whether the new culture fits you, find out about it."

Peter J. says he knew for nearly two years that he'd been targeted as someone to be phased out of the organization. But he felt helpless to do anything about it as circumstances picked him up and carried him along.

In fact, there were things he could have done, Smye says. But first, he had to decide whether the new rules worked for him. If they didn't and he had decided to leave to find another employer, he could have asked the company for counselling help. "People generally need help to move through the transition," she explains.

Had he decided he really wanted to stay, Peter could have had what Smye calls a "tough love conversation." He could have gone to his superior and said: "I feel that people think (or you think) I can't adjust to the new culture. And I want to. What do I need to do to prove it?"

Smye's suggestions, though targeted at employees, are equally valid for those looking for work. Set goals, take the initiative, talk to people, keep an open mind — good advice for anyone trying to find a niche in today's job market.

Change is both traumatic and challenging for everybody involved. Senior managers who introduce it have no easier a time than those who have to implement it. In the 1990s, however, it's simply not avoidable. Everybody in the workplace needs to prepare for change and learn how to manage it.

"Remember, this is your life," advises Smye. "Take charge of it."

Just over a year ago, after working for the same company for 10 years, I was demoted and laid off. My job search has been long and gruelling. I keep bumping into people who work for my old employer who ask: 'Aren't you working, YET?' They also stress that some of the people who were let go with me have been called back. How do you reply? I'm tired of defending myself.

Janis Foord Kirk
Career Monitor

AND IN REPLY

The insensitivity of people who are working toward people who aren't amazes me. Don't let them get to you. Smile, and respond to their bad manners by saying something like: "Well, the job market is tight these days, as you know, and I'm being fairly selective. The job I held toward the end of my time at XYZ company wasn't a particularly good fit for me. I want to be certain to find the right place this time." Then move on.

Chapter 3

DOING THE
SPADE WORK

SUSAN TODD

When jobs are scarce, dig deeper

I n the best of times — which, everyone agrees, these aren't —jobs are so plentiful you sometimes trip over them. Take this conversation overheard at a social gathering late in 1988: "Kevin! I was hoping you'd be here. A buddy of mine called yesterday and he's looking for a cost accountant. I didn't want to give him your name until I talked to you."

Ah, for the abundance of the late '80s. Those days are gone, however, at least for now. These days, jobs are buried deep. You have to dig to find them. And that means research.

Webster's Dictionary defines research as "careful, patient, systematic, diligent inquiry or examination in some field of knowledge."

Careful, patient, systematic, diligent — sounds like a lot of hard work, and it is. There's no getting around it. Research of any kind is hard work, and job market research is no exception.

> Research is how you get the information you need to make intelligent choices and decisions.

Still, if you're out of work and struggling to find a new job, if you're new to an area (or to the workforce) and wanting to get a sense of the business community, if you're changing fields (or thinking about it), research is how you get the information you need to make intelligent choices and decisions.

Though it might sound tedious, once you're into it, research becomes involving, interesting and, ultimately, rewarding in career terms. It gives you information and, in subtle ways, information bestows confidence on the person who has it. In the job market, you'll appear informed and knowledgeable. As you talk to people gathering information and giving it, you'll impress them. They may even want to hire you.

At its most dynamic, research is a circuitous, yet progressive, process of reading and talking to people. In *What Color Is Your Parachute?* (Ten Speed Press), Richard Bolles puts it this way: "You read until you need to talk to someone because you can't find more in books; then you talk to people until you know you need to get back and do some more reading."

Whichever research method you use, the goal is always the same — to gather relevant, current and accurate data. With career and job market research, an additional goal is the building of lists — lists of companies and organizations of interest to you, lists of people who may be able to help in your quest.

Libraries, the storage banks for most printed material, are the logical places to start. Learning to use a library will demand some of that careful, patient, systematic diligence mentioned earlier. It will also test your perseverance. Don't become discouraged if your first visit isn't productive.

Librarians can be a wonderful resource. But before discussing your needs with one, make sure you're clear about what it is you're researching.

Pulling together a list of philanthropic organizations in your area will be a different research project than if you're looking into the various careers available to someone with a philanthropic bent. And different, again, from the research you'd do into the activities of the local branch of the Canadian Cancer Society before sending a resume.

No matter what information you're after, a librarian can point you to the right resource. Directories list organizations by industry, location and specialty. All sorts of publications can help you investigate specific careers, the most extensive Canadian resource being the Canadian Classification and Dictionary of Occupations (CCDO). Specific information on large public companies and well-known organizations is also available.

If you're not a practised researcher, start at the business desk of your regional library. Get a sense of what's available. If it's a small branch, you'll no doubt find it limiting after a time and decide to move on to a major library.

Generally speaking, the larger the library, the more extensive the bank of information. Check as well with colleges and universities in your area. They often have career or reference libraries open to the public on request. Some large associations also have libraries.

And look for resources in your community.

Martha, who hopes to work close to home, made several calls and visits to the municipal offices and Chambers of Commerce in the four regional centres within a 40-mile radius of her place. She now has directories listing all companies and organizations conducting business in the area. One afternoon a week, she drives through industrial and commercial areas noting the names of companies to investigate.

Ongoing reading — "intuitive reading," it's sometimes called — of industry-specific publications and journals is an essential part of any career research. Being well informed about current trends and events in your field will help you anticipate opportunities and stay ahead of the pack.

Become involved in the industry in which you're building your career. Join associations, take in trade shows and conferences. In virtually every field, technology and the changing marketplace are affecting present and potential job opportunities. Keeping abreast of trends like these will give you an edge.

Few people are natural researchers. In fact, the kind of laborious digging required to get at buried or "hidden jobs" is generally saved for a thesis, or a special project assigned by your boss. When it comes to job market research, there's no time frame, no mark to achieve, no one to assign you. Nonetheless, research projects like these are as important. They directly affect your future well-being.

Ask the experts

"I attribute what little I know to my not having been ashamed to ask for information, and to my rule of conversing with all descriptions of men on those topics that form their own peculiar professions and pursuits. "

— John Locke

Knowledge builds from experience. It's a common observation, and as far back as the 17th century, people like philosopher John Locke were commenting on its importance to personal development.

In these career-minded times, talking to people about their own "peculiar professions and pursuits" has acquired official status, at least in job-search terms. "Informational interviewing," it's called.

The premise behind interviews of this kind is that the most direct way to research a particular field is to talk to the experts — people who spend their days working in it.

Henry, a middle manager in benefit administration, "fell into" his line of work. For nearly 20 years he "got by," he says, never excelling, never blundering seriously either. Nonetheless, he was one of nearly 50 people let go when his employer "reorganized."

Instinctively, Henry tried to replace the job he lost. When he couldn't and months passed, he began to think about a change of career.

Through a process of self-examination, Henry slowly became aware that, although he enjoys the personnel field, he's far happier working with people than he is working with statistics and data. He decided to turn his sights to training and development, perhaps even recruiting.

Though he has some understanding of these areas, Henry needs more information. Which of his existing skills are transferable? What skills and training should he add to his credentials? Where can he get the best training? What opportunities exist once he has it? How can he best present himself — his goals, his background — on a resume, and in interviews?

Narida, too, is in need of information, though for different reasons. She's moving to Calgary. Her husband has been offered a job there, a promotion. The family decided he couldn't turn it down.

An advertising manager in the retail industry, Narida is well-established and respected in Toronto. She now faces the daunting prospect of leaving her job behind to start over in a new city, in an unknown business community, in a time of economic uncertainty.

Once in Calgary, Narida will need to develop a clear sense of the advertising industry there, how it functions, who the major players are, what companies are growing or changing and may be in need of additional staff.

Before interviewing for information, she'll have to assess who has it. Projects like this begin with a list of people known to be respected professionals in their field.

Henry, well-connected after years of working in one industry in one city, will have something of a head start. By phoning and talking to people he knows, he can put together such a list with little difficulty.

Narida, on the other hand, will be starting from scratch — no contacts, no obvious place to begin.

"Never let a little thing like that stop you," says career consultant Bill Nolan. According to Nolan, you can get whatever information you need by using a technique he calls "the advice call."

"The advice call can help people gain access to business people, executives, politicians, managers and entrepreneurs," Nolan says.

Those starting from scratch, as Narida is, begin the process with the type of research mentioned earlier. Library research on the field under investigation, together with intuitive reading of business journals and industry-specific publications, will provide the information needed to make a list of leaders in any industry.

Once that list is compiled, Nolan advises "a few practice runs with people you know and respect."

Just getting through on the phone can be a major hurdle, so "be polite, firm, confident and persistent," he advises. "Never leave your name and number. Make a note to call back."

When she gets her expert on the phone, Narida will have to introduce herself, briefly describe her background, and say something like: "I'm new to the city and spending some time talking to people in this field before launching a job search. I'm calling successful people like yourself to seek their advice. Would you be able to spend 20 minutes with me, some time next week?"

Not everyone will agree to see her, of course, but some will. And slowly, her base of information, industry-specific and area-specific, will grow.

But what if the expert gets confused, or resists her request?

"Point out that you're not selling anything, you're not looking for a job and that you'll only take 20 minutes of their time," says Nolan.

When they do meet, Narida should provide a "capsule overview" of her career, closing with her move to Calgary, he suggests. Then she should say: "Put yourself in my shoes. With that background, what would you do?'"

Though an advice call should always begin with a general request of this sort, you can get more specific about your plans as the meeting progresses, Nolan says. Narida's approach might be something like: "One of the fields I'm considering is direct mail. What would your thoughts be on that?"

> "Judge a man
> by his questions,
> rather than his
> answers."
>
> — *Voltaire*

Be sure to "place no restrictions whatsoever on the reply," Nolan advises. "Be deliberately open-ended. Listen carefully. You may get a piece of advice that will stand you in good stead for the rest of your life."

As with conversations of any kind, each interview will be different. Nonetheless, there are some common factors. Should you decide, like Henry and Narida, to give informational interviewing or advice calls a try, here are some basic rules:

• Keep in mind at all times that these are business meetings, with busy people. If you've asked for 20 minutes of their time, take no more than that. Plan carefully how to make the best use of that time.

• Don't launch into an interview unprepared, with general, unfocused questions. It was Voltaire who said: "Judge a man by his questions, rather than his answers." If your questions aren't intelligent and well researched, you'll have missed the hidden opportunity behind informational interviews — to impress people in your field who have the potential to become "contacts," and who may know of jobs.

• NEVER, EVER attempt to turn an informational interview into a job interview. If it becomes obvious your true reason for making this contact was to say "please hire me," you lose all credibility.

• After each interview, follow up with a thank-you note or letter.

Interviewing selected people to get information and advice is an effective career exploration technique. Prepare yourself well, tenaciously seek out experts, conduct professional meetings with them, and you can get a head start in a new career, a new city, or a new specialty within your field.

Meeting successful people and gaining their insight are the main benefits, Nolan says. "They boost your self-confidence and help you build an optimistic view of the future. You can sharpen your interview skills. And advice calls often lead to referrals and job leads."

Once the contact has been made, be professional and you'll maintain it. Review what was said in the meeting in your thank-you letter and express your appreciation for your host's time and suggestions.

Nolan, a strong advocate of advice calls, describes them as a "dynamic career management tool." They are equally effective for people who are "unemployed, employed in their own business, or just leaving their own business and going into corporate Canada, or vice versa.

"It's a versatile technique that's been around for thousands of years," he adds. "If you go back into Proverbs you'll find it."

"Proverbs?" I ask skeptically. "Can you give us a proverb that promotes advice calls?"

"You bet," says Nolan without missing a beat. "Plans fail for lack of counsel. But with many advisers, they succeed."

TIP

"Think of the advice call as a business meeting, not an interview," advises entrepreneur Vicki V. "Always go well prepared with a list of questions. Ask: 'How is the business run? How do you pick your employees? How do you train people? How do you build your mission statement? How do you plan to grow? What is your three to five-year plan?' Ask: 'What does the emerging global economy mean to you? How will it change your business?'"

IN MEMORIAM
Bill Nolan, a career management expert quoted here, died in 1991. Bill gave of his time and expertise generously whenever asked. He is missed by those who knew him and worked with him.

Chapter 4

TACKLING THE JOB MARKET

ALFRED WONG

Finding work may be the hardest job of all

The numbers are staggering. So many people can't find work, and a vast pool of human potential is lying dormant, waiting for the economic engine to turn over and catch.

"Most people are quite accommodating and sympathetic," says Bjorn, "but they say nothing is happening, and won't be for the foreseeable future. They say they'll keep me on file."

"I know I would do a good job if someone would just hire me," says Tom. "But they don't seem to want to."

"They're sympathetic," says Jeff, "but there's nothing. They're looking at themselves and worrying that they may be next."

Today, more than ever, it's tough being unemployed. Most everyone who is works hard at the job of finding a job. Despite their very best efforts, many can't seem to make headway. Inevitably, their frustration grows.

> "Most people are sympathetic, but they say nothing is happening."

Three men, all from the hard-hit manufacturing sector, discuss what it's like to be out of work. By all accounts, these are hard-working men with good track records. Like so many others, they're caught, victims of an industry and a workplace in the throes of a major restructuring.

Bjorn

Since arriving in Canada from Sweden in the late 1970s, Bjorn has worked as a buyer and purchasing agent. A relentless job seeker with a good background in his field and a strong resume, he's been looking for work for more than six months.

"Manufacturing and distribution are very, very slow right now," he says, having made almost 700 contacts and come up with nothing. "Everybody is so short of cash these days and so worried about the future. "They just don't spend. They make do with what they have."

Wisely, Bjorn has been taking some career-related courses.

And he's been talking to people in his industry, trying to get a sense of where it's going and how he fits in to it. "Be patient," was the advice he got. "Eventually, the waiting game will pay off."

"People have told me that purchasing and inventory control is very important to the bottom line," Bjorn says. "For six months to a year, I'm going to have a tough time, they said, but when industry starts hiring again, they're going to need purchasing people."

For now, like so many others in similar circumstances, all he can do is continue to search and try not to become overwhelmed by the growing frustration.

Tom

Like Bjorn, Tom has a positive attitude and an impressive work record. "What frustrates me more than anything is that I know I'm a valuable person when I work for a company," says Tom, a veteran salesman. He's been looking for work for 10 months now. The 400 to 500 resumes he's sent out have generated maybe 35 interviews, he says. But so far, no job offers.

"Part of it, I think, is my age," speculates Tom, 55. "It's that, and the competition. There are so many people out there looking for a job. Why would they hire someone my age, when they can find someone 25, with a college education?"

What he offers an employer, Tom says, is loyalty, maturity and years of experience. He can't quite believe they're not enough to get him a job.

Jeff

At 37, Jeff, despite his college education, is not having an easier time.

For more than 10 years, Jeff worked as a buyer and merchandiser in food retail and distribution. "When I chose my field years ago, I was told, 'get into the food industry, people always have to eat,'" he says with a weary chuckle. "Did they have that wrong."

Since losing his job last January, Jeff has contacted 200 to 300 people with resumes and phone calls, he says.

"I want to work," Jeff says. "I'm not used to being at home. I'm being Mr. Mom, these days. I'm busy. But it's a job I want."

In the minds of those without it, work is almost as valuable as the income it represents. Jeff has little sympathy when he hears employed people carping about meagre wage increases. "I think, how can they do this? Don't they realize they have a job, a *job*. They have somewhere to go every day. They can come home at night and feel respectable."

A common thread runs through these stories. Work validates Tom, Bjorn and Jeff. It makes each of them feel worthwhile and connected to the society at large. Without it, they feel empty and stifled. As the months of unemployment pass, inevitably their confidence ebbs.

TIP

"Throughout your job search, keep a diary of all your activities every day," suggests human resource consultant Sandy Wise. "Use it to note things like who you've called, and letters you've written. That way, at the end of each day, or each week, you can look back and feel that you've accomplished something."

Deciphering the job ads

Answering a job advertisement during times of high unemployment is a little like shooting an arrow into a vast abyss. A single ad can draw hundreds of replies. Applications that aren't targeted to the job, that don't address the specific needs of the employer who wrote the ad, are easily overlooked.

But with forethought and effort, you can create an application that hits the mark — and get an interview.

Consider what it's like to be on the receiving end of hundreds of job applications. Someone has to go through each one to assess whether there's a potential "fit." When dealing with an overwhelming stack of resumes, the initial screening of any particular one often takes no more than 30 seconds. If your written work doesn't grab the reader's attention in that short space of time, it's set aside.

And when that happens, you've just wasted what an unemployed manager recently estimated to be "an hour or two of time and maybe three or four dollars in materials and postage."

This doesn't mean, of course, that you shouldn't apply to job ads. They are, and always will be, an excellent source of job leads. It does mean, however, that your application has to compete with possibly hundreds of others and that you need to apply accordingly.

Learning to read ads objectively with a discerning eye is a valuable job search skill. There are ways to assess such ads to see whether there's enough of a "fit" to warrant responding. And when there is, there are ways to make that abundantly clear in your application.

Under close scrutiny, a job ad — which in many ways is a mini-job description — can provide a wealth of information about the job, the company and even the corporate culture.

Generally, a recruitment ad opens with a "short introductory paragraph that talks about the benefits of working for a particular organization," explains Nadia Bailey, a senior writer with Day Advertising Group, a recruitment advertising firm.

"It will then outline the responsibilities of the position and the qualifications," Bailey says. "The closing paragraph is a 'call to action' telling people how to apply."

Ads list "four or five of the most important responsibilities and four or five of the most important qualifications," says Bailey. "It would stand to reason that you have to have them in order to apply," she adds.

The wording of an ad can tell you what the employer's priorities are, says Sandra Higgins, director of client services for Bernard Hodes Advertising, another firm specializing in recruitment advertising.

In most ads, there are *must haves* and *will ideally haves*, says Higgins. "If you can come up with all of them, you're in like Flynn. If you have the *must haves* and not the *ideally*, you may get the interview, but you may not get the job."

> There are ways to assess whether there's enough of a "fit" to warrant responding.

When reading ads, "check also to see if the mood and tone of the ad matches your own," Nadia Bailey suggests. Ads that are dry and technical, for example, can tell you something about the company and what's important to them, she says.

Assessing a recruitment ad like this can also help you apply for a job in a specific, and memorable, way. Underline all the requirements of the job as stated in the ad. Write them down on the left side of a sheet of paper. Now, be objective. On the right side of the page, note your experience and training as it relates to those requirements. Can you see a fit?

In better employment markets, it's worth applying if you can meet 60 per cent of the requirements. In tough times, you'd better have 75 per cent. "Otherwise don't bother," says Higgins.

Even when your background matches the job requirements, don't assume it will be immediately obvious to anyone reading your resume. Creative job seekers will take time to interpret their backgrounds in terms of the employer's needs.

It's not the application that gets the interview, but the quality of the application. Every mailed resume must be accompanied by a covering letter — never a form letter or one that reads like one.

The letter is your chance to explain, clearly, how your background fits the requirements of the job as outlined in the ad. Be specific. Talk about the contributions you can make to the organization.

In many ways, this is where you begin to anticipate the needs of your employer-to-be. One employer put it this way: "A resume tells me what someone has done in the past. The covering letter tells me how that relates to me and what they can do for me."

Deciphering job ads is an art. Anyone new to the job hunting game will find it tough. It will be fairly easy to assess yourself against what Sandra Higgins calls "hard qualifications — your degree, the number of years you've put in, your technical knowledge."

The other terms used in ads are often "buzzwords," Higgins says. Because they're highly subjective, it can be more difficult to assess yourself against them.

Understanding the terms

"Hands on." "Bottom line orientation." "Dynamic."

The buzzwords of job advertisements are commonplace. To anyone seeking work, they are crucial to an understanding of what the employer is looking for. But how well are they understood?

Not very well, according to one job seeker, who wrote to ask: "What exactly do employers mean when they use terms like 'hands-on' or 'professional designation or equivalent'? A better understanding of the different terms used in advertisements would benefit job seekers, employers and readers at large."

Career Monitor asked Higgins and Bailey to help compile a glossary of such terms.

Hands on
A person who rolls up his or her shirt sleeves and gets involved. A "doer."

Professional designation or equivalent
A professional accreditation or other training and/or years of experience in a particular field to compensate.

Excellent oral and communication skills
One who can easily get a point across, who speaks clearly and is easily understood.

Results-oriented
One who is motivated to see a project through to completion; one who is focused on the objective and makes sure it is met.

Problem solver
One who can look objectively at a problem, examine a situation from several angles, and come up with a solution.

Required to liaise with
One who is in contact, on the phone or in person, with a variety of people.

A strong technical understanding
One who can take the back off a machine and find out what makes it work; one who understands the mechanical workings of a machine or piece of equipment.

Dynamic
Someone with a strong, extroverted personality.

Self-motivated
One who doesn't wait to be told what to do; one who takes the initiative, who sees what has to be done and simply does it.

Change manager
One who can help others manage the transition from the old way of doing things to the new way.

People skills
The skills of one who deals effectively with people, convincing or encouraging them to do what's required.

Progressive experience
One who has advanced steadily within a specific industry or field.

Promotable
One who can come into a job, assimilate what's required, become proficient at it, and then be ready to move up.

World class
One of the best in the world, committed to excellence.

Global view
One who has strong awareness of the international scene.

Strong team orientation/team oriented
Someone who thrives as a member of a team; one who is able to work successfully as part of a group.

Able to work independently/without supervision/with minimal supervision.
One driven by an internal challenge; one who doesn't need to be assigned or to have someone checking on their efforts.

Creative problem solver/or thinker
One who can look at a situation that isn't working and come up with a better way.

Confident
One who will speak up and state his or her case.

Provide technical support
To use one's technical abilities to support others who don't have such abilities.

Crisis manager
One able to deal effectively with the unexpected; one who can think quickly and come up with a professional response in an emergency; one who can mediate and manage people in a crisis.

Bottom-line orientation
One who can get the job done in a timely and cost-effective manner; one who's aware of what's required to make a profit.

Able to set priorities/or prioritize assignments
One who can sort through a number of assignments and identify those that can wait and those that need to be handled immediately.

A big-picture team player
One able to develop an intelligent overview of the situation and make the team function to manage it.

An aggressive self-starter
One who can walk into a situation and whip it into shape.

Effective decision-making skills
The skills of one who is able to make decisions and not be gathering information forever.

Analytical skills
The ability to take information, digest it, and come up with conclusions.

This is not an exhaustive list, and the meanings given are not carved in stone. Phrases are coined regularly, Bailey and Higgins say, and tend to change according to the needs of the organization and the job.

Beyond the want ads

Just before lunch, 20 office workers are invited to a meeting in the board room. It's a busy day. "What now?" one asks another in the corridor. "I've got to get that report in the mail." The personnel manager, walking by, hears the question. She offers only a tight smile.

On the executive floor, Joe's secretary walks softly on two-inch plush. "Mr. Namin wants to come down and see you in about 10 minutes," she says. Joe looks at her quizzically. She shrugs, and shakes her head.

About a hundred production workers are asked to meet in the cafeteria after their shift. This has never happened before and as they gather, most of them have a heavy feeling in the pit of their stomachs. A grim-faced plant manager enters the room.

> "It's not the best person for the job who gets it. It's the person who knows best how to look for work."

"We're moving south" ... "We're cutting back"..."Your services are no longer required." Scenes like these have become commonplace in the early '90s.

For those already among the ranks of the jobless, news of such developments simply adds to the discouragement. With so many jobs going down the drain, why get up and spend another day looking for work? Numbers like that make it easy to roll over and go back to sleep.

Yes, the job market is tight. Yes, the numbers are worrisome. But it's not true that "there's nothing out there."

Some organizations are doing just fine. Some are even expanding. People retire, they change jobs if a better one comes their way. Although the pace of activity is slow, new business *is* being generated. Decisions to hire, however long they seem to take, *are* still being made.

"It's distracting to think `there are no jobs for me,'" says career consultant John Hamilton. "There are jobs in any market, there are needs in any market. It's a matter of being better at finding them."

"It's not the best person for the job who gets it," he adds. "It's the person who knows best how to look for work."

Whether that work is in an office, a factory or on the executive floor, it will help to understand one basic fact. There isn't, as people often assume, one single job market. There are two. One is visible, the other hidden.

Think of want ads, employment agencies and recruiting firms. That's the visible job market. In recent years it has taken a beating. The number of jobs advertised in the help-wanted pages and career sections of newspapers across North America has dropped steadily. Recruiters report fewer jobs coming their way, too.

> "Seventy-five per cent of job opportunities are found in the hidden job market."

Most people look for work in this visible job market, so the competition is stiff. One recruiter reported recently that a single job ad can draw anywhere from 200 to 1,000 replies these days.

Since the hidden job market is harder to get at, not as many people look for work in it. And yet, according to author Ronald Krannich in his book *Re-Careering In Turbulent Times* (Impact Publishing), that's where all the action is.

"It is this job market that should occupy most of your attention," he writes. "Although the hidden job market lacks a formal structure, 75 per cent or more of all job opportunities are found here."

The hidden job market is the vast underbelly of the labor market. Except to the most resourceful of job seekers, it's a mysterious place; a vast labyrinth of shadowy job opportunities that always seem to get filled by word of mouth.

In fact, it's accessible to everyone. With tenacity, creativity and hard work, you can wage a campaign to opens doors in it. While it's not necessarily always flourishing, it tends to be more active in a slow economy than the visible job market.

A hidden job is a gleam in some manager's eye. The organization needs additional staff, but nothing has been done about it. Advertising and recruiting fees are high and it's difficult to justify spending money during troublesome times. If you show up on that manager's doorstep and have what it takes to fill that company's needs, you've found an opportunity in the hidden job market.

To find hidden jobs, you have to keep digging — persistence is key.

The foundation of a creative job search campaign in the hidden market is a list of employers for whom you'd like to work and who may have the kind of job you seek. This list won't come together in one sitting. It develops over time. You need to research, talk to people, read, do more research, and then talk to more people.

It's an involved process, yes. But those who muster the energy to follow it through find "it has terrific payoffs," says psychologist and career specialist Elaine Cooper.

Networking

Most people come to the networking process "kicking and screaming," Cooper says. "The anxiety is natural. Nobody finds networking easy. You need to feel the fear and do it anyway."

Once you begin, you'll find it happens on several different levels.

At first, networking means talking to people you know, even slightly, and asking for information, leads, advice and referrals. When putting your list of contacts together, "don't overlook anybody," Cooper says. "Start with people who are easiest for you and then weave your way out."

In his book *Jeff Allen's Best: Get The Interview* (John Wiley & Sons, Inc.), Jeffrey Allen advises: "Don't be too selective.

"You're not inviting them over for a job club meeting, only writing down their name and number. Then cast your net to find out what they know

> "Start with people who are easiest for you and then weave your way out."

about companies that are hiring and jobs you'd like to do."

At the same time, cast your net for referrals. In a tough job market you have to "dig a bit deeper," says industrial sociologist Sy Eber. "Look for secondary and tertiary referrals from your primary network. Don't back off too quickly. Don't take no as the final answer. When someone can't help you, ask if they'll send you on to someone who can."

As Cooper suggests, the networking process is difficult for everyone. Still, people who are naturally outgoing are going to have an easier time than those who aren't, she says. "Introverts have the same needs but will have to find a different approach. It has nothing to do with social skills or with liking people. It has to do with interpersonal comfort levels."

If you're less outgoing, you might consider volunteering or becoming involved in cultural or church activities, suggests Cooper. This way you can meet like-minded people and make what she calls "a task-related contact."

Information gathering

The commodity of exchange in networking is information. The more you have, the more effective your approach will be.

As noted earlier, the business sections of local newspapers, national business magazines and industry-specific publications can provide a sense of what's happening regionally and nationally.

But don't stop there. While most job searches are regionally based, a complex set of factors affects local job markets.

"We are living in a global village," says Elaine Cooper. "It's important to understand the international market. Read publications like the Wall Street Journal, The Economist, Forbes and The Guardian. Look at what's happening abroad.

"Stay current," she advises. "Then, as you network and meet people, you've got the ability to converse in a broader sense."

Directory research

Possibly the most tedious part of a creative job-search campaign is poring through business directories looking for leads. "It's a lot of hard work," acknowledges Sy Eber. Still, "directories are helpful in terms of categorizing information, getting leads and new ideas," he says.

Municipalities put out business directories. So do specific industries and specialty areas within industries. Talk to a librarian at the business desk of a major library to find out what directories exist for organizations that fit into your target group.

Before approaching any of the corporate officers listed in these directories, phone and verify the information. "Things change quickly

Though seldom used as a job-search technique, the drop-in approach sometimes works. You develop a list of companies, get the name of the decision maker and drop in, hoping to find that person has time to see you.

It's a time-consuming way to look for work. Still, if your telephone skills and writing skills aren't strong, it can be the most effective way to put the word out about your job search.

The drop-in method of job search works best in smaller centres where businesses operate in a more informal way. It might also be the way to approach people in industrial settings or on work sites.

If you feel it would work in your particular situation, arm yourself with a stack of resumes, plan in advance the basics of what it is you'd like to say about yourself, and hit the road.

Whichever job search method you decide to choose, in today's economic climate, persistence is key. You have to keep digging, keep asking for referrals. The jobs come up, we're told, at the third level of referral. This means finding the time and the patience to contact the person whose name was given to you by the person you were directed to by the first contact you made.

In tight job markets, especially, you have to become something of a detective, like Tony.

A chemical engineer, Tony had been looking for work for six months when he spotted a trailer truck with the name of a chemical company on its side as he was driving home one evening.

"I made a U-turn and followed the truck," Tony recalls. "It was a spontaneous thing. I'd been through the Scott's Directory and all the other directories and I didn't recognize the name. I just reacted."

Tony copied the phone number from the side of the truck. The next day, he called the company, got a name and address and sent a letter. Within a week, he had an interview. Although he got some work from that contact, it unfortunately didn't turn into a full-time job.

Ever resourceful, Tony's still at it. "Recently, I drove by a company, and again, I didn't recognize the name," he says. "I checked all the directories and the phone books and it wasn't listed anywhere.

"What I'm going to have to do is drive over there, walk into the office, and get some information."

I'm leaving this city. I've got a couple of places in mind, but few resources to visit any of them. How can I research them from here?

Janis Foord Kirk
Career Monitor

AND IN REPLY

Write the Chamber of Commerce in each centre and ask to have an information package sent to you. Write the major newspaper in each centre as well. Ask how to arrange a mail subscription. Try to read these papers at least a couple of times each week, and you'll get a sense of the community, the issues of importance to it, and who the major players are. You'll also get a look at some of the jobs available in that area and some of the local employers.

Write as well to the local municipal economic or business development office. Most of them publish industrial directories that list the companies doing business in that area.

At a book store or library, get hold of Richard Bolles's *What Color Is Your Parachute? (Ten Speed Press)*. In Appendix E, at the back of the book, is a section called *How Do I Survey A Place That Is Far Away?* It outlines the various things you can do to familiarize yourself with a new centre before moving there.

Create your own job

A lengthy track record can make you an expert in your field. Still, lots of experts are out of work these days. There don't seem to be enough jobs to go around.

Does this mean years of experience no longer matter in the job market of the '90s? Not at all. It's simply that out-of-work experts often don't know how to persuade employers to hire them.

Even in tight fiscal times, it can be done. There are ways to create your own job — if not a full-time position, perhaps a contract or consulting job.

But you'll need selling skills to pull it off.

"Our whole economy is based on soliciting business," says Andrea Moses, director of Powerbase Consultants, a Toronto sales training firm. "A job search is no different. If you want to get things happening for you, you have to solicit business."

Moses, author of *Street Smart Selling*, believes sales techniques can be applied readily to job hunting.

"Street smart selling is about persuasion," Moses explains. "Whether you're looking for a job, promoting your ideas or selling a product, it's all the same. You're influencing someone to do what you want."

Moses's concept of selling is based on the theory of self-interest. People will buy from you (or hire you) only if it's in their interest to do so, she says.

> "You have to tie your skills into a company's ultimate goal, which is to increase profit."

And in the business community, she adds, self-interest and profit are inexorably intertwined.

"You have to tie your skills into a company's ultimate goal, which is to increase profit," Moses says.

The entire process begins with preparation, which bores most people but must be done, she says.

"Do your homework on yourself. Look at the jobs you've had. Identify what you were able to accomplish. Identify some unique advantage you have. Sell yourself on the concept that you can offer something to a company that no one else can."

At all times, keep the profit motive in mind, she advises.

"How can your skills be translated into dollars and cents for a company? You're either going to bring in income or save expenses. Can you increase sales? Can you increase the productivity of people? Can you increase the company's visibility?"

Develop a list of companies that could use your expertise, by reading business pages of newspapers, business magazines and journals. If a company in your industry is in trouble, "there'll be problems you can solve," Moses says. "If it's doing well, you can help them achieve their goals."

Your approach will be unique if you spend time thinking about what a company's needs are, what you can do for it, she says. "Most people don't think like that; most think about what a company can do for them."

Contact the vice-president of the department or area in which you would work. These executives generally have a discretionary budget, she explains.

The script of what Moses calls an "introductory call" would go something like this:

"My name is........... I'm calling to introduce myself. I'm a computer expert (or marketing expert, administrative expert, etc.). I've been reading about your firm and your plans (or problems) and I can predict that you might need someone with top-notch skills in this area."

Then, give a one-sentence statement of the results you've produced. "In my work, I've helped companies................."

Next, start asking questions: What are you doing now in this area? How is it working out? What are the strengths of your people? What are their limitations?

Maintain this question-asking role until you find a problem you can solve, Moses says.

"You have to think of your product (in this case, you) as a solution to a problem," she explains. "The key, the crux of selling, of whether you get what you want or you don't, is understanding that you're a solution to a problem."

Once you've identified the problem, summarize it. Suggest that you can help solve it.

At this stage, she says, you'll no doubt run into the standard objection: "We don't have the budget."

Respond to that objection in terms of "dollars and cents," Moses advises. Say something like: "I understand that you don't have a budget for this, but if I could prove to you that by hiring me as a consultant, I could save you money, would you be interested?"

It will be difficult to say no to that. Request a meeting. In it, don't attempt to sell yourself, spend most of your time "exploring the situation in depth," she advises. Get a clearer sense of the problem, then ask to make a presentation to all staff affected by it.

"By now, the person has some connection to you," Moses says. "And you're not being compared to hundreds of other candidates."

Only about five to 10 per cent of people are truly "street smart," Moses estimates. But selling skills can be learned.

"You may not have them today," Moses says, "But that doesn't mean you can't develop them over time."

For people with expertise but no job, the lack of selling skills could be the only thing holding them back.

The "unconventional Arts" — a last-ditch solution

Sometimes a job search succeeds, not because of months of slogging, but through a sudden stroke of brilliance. Whenever that happens, it's inspirational. Take the story of Theresa Arts.

After several years of looking, Arts finally landed a job. Not just any job, either. "The one I wanted," she says. "In a high-tech industry, and at more than the dollars I asked for."

She wrote *Career Monitor* to pass on her job-hunting technique, "a strange method that was successful after less than six weeks.... Even if one

> "When something's not working, we have to become more creative."

other individual finds a job using my method, this letter to you will have been successful," Arts wrote.

In the late '80s, after a successful climb up the corporate ladder, Arts was one of the many middle managers displaced by corporate restructuring. She looked "off and on" for work for several years but, other than a six-month contract job, had little luck getting her career back on track.

For the most part, Arts, 50, followed conventional job-search wisdom. "I had a polished two-page resume with a one-page individualized covering letter," she explains. Faithfully, she answered ads and worked her network. But nothing happened.

"When something's not working, we have to become more creative," she says.

As a first step, Arts researched her target job market. Using a business directory, she got the names of all manufacturing companies of 50 to 300 employees in her area. "I sent out about 600 letters, each addressed to the CEO," she recalls.

Theresa Arts and her abilities literally leap off the page of her letter. It begins: "Please scrap this letter if you don't need a top-notch right hand, anywhere in your organization. But, if at this point you've decided to read on (it will take you three minutes), along the way imagine what I can do for you. Because, over the last 20 years I have:...."

Then, using point form, Arts lists, in "deliberate and diverse random order," 51 things she has done throughout her career. What's impressive about this list, about the whole letter, in fact, is its objectivity. Still, each point is positive, or at least worded in a positive way. Things like:
- lobbied for change
- related to CEO and mail clerk with equal ease and respect
- managed company funds as if they were my own
- endured posturing prima donnas

Arts takes care to note several "downsides," as well:
- petrified about public speaking
- recognize the need for, but prefer not to engage in, corporate gamesmanship
- always want to know the why of things.

When writing the letter, Arts "laced it with common sense, and good-natured, down-to-earth humor," she says. "I used no dates, company names, positions held, courageous achievements, and no lies."

Here's a sentence that illustrates her style: "I abhor mediocrity, take initiative, do not wilt, cannot be flustered, work well with minimum supervision, have more than two hands (and eyes in the back of my head) and am a team player."

The letter closes with: "You've done me the courtesy of giving me three minutes. I thank you. Now. If you think you can use me, invest another 30 seconds in a call...."

And call they did. Over the following month and a half, Arts had one to four interviews each business day, she says — "armed, of course, with a pristine resume, impeccable references and other backup materials."

One of the calls came from Michael Greenberg, a neurosurgeon turned businessman who is president and CEO of a company that develops and manufactures 3-D imaging equipment for the medical field.

Greenberg's account of his circumstances when Arts' letter crossed his desk sounds like an narrative from a bygone era. Business was booming, he says, and he was "swamped. I needed an assistant. However I was so busy, I was despairing of having the time to find one. And there was her letter. It seemed like a godsend."

In fact, Greenberg was so busy, he called Arts to say, "I'd like to meet you, but I'm flying in tonight and out again on Monday morning. It will have to be several weeks from now."

"I asked him what time his plane arrived," Arts recalls with a chuckle. "And, when he told me, I said, `I'll pick you up.'"

Which she did. Their first meeting was followed by several others, and within a couple of weeks, a job offer was made. At no point during that time, did Arts have any competition for the job.

Arts' letter intrigued Greenberg, made him want to meet her, he says. "It was obviously written by someone who had a lot of intelligence, who had style and personality. It so happens that the particular personality, as expressed in that letter, I found appealing."

Not everyone can pull off an unorthodox job search of this sort. But if you have a strong sense of your own skills, your strengths and your weaknesses, if you can develop a clear understanding of who might need them, perhaps it's worth a try. Be careful, however, to be certain you can deliver, as Arts has been able to do.

"My first impressions of her have been reinforced over the past month," Greenberg says. "Theresa's genuine. She has the goods."

TIP

Every job campaign will be a long series of NOs, followed by a YES. "That is the usual, standard, universal job campaign," writes Tom Jackson in *Guerrilla Tactics For The Job Market* (Bantam Books). "The more willing you are to explore new fields and directions, the more NOs you will create."

Seek out the NOs, Jackson advises. Don't let them stop you. They are an inevitable part of any job search and the more of them you get, the closer you are to the ultimate YES.

Chapter 5

STAYING POSITIVE

SUSAN TODD

Keeping your spirits up

Remaining strong, dedicated and confident in a depressing job market takes conscious effort.

"Sometimes I get down when my job search efforts result in reject letters, or I hear nothing at all," writes would-be marketer Gail W.

Says Ruth L., who's been knocking on doors in the publishing field: "You have to constantly fend off discouragement, disillusionment and falling self-esteem."

From the letters of these two women, both aspiring to new careers, come valuable tips on how to keep yourself up throughout a lengthy job search.

For the past year, Gail W. has been writing letters and sending off resumes. "I sometimes wonder if I made a mistake when I decided to give up my career to raise a family," Gail writes. "I thought that obtaining a university degree at the same time would overcome any negative effects."

So far, this hasn't proved to be the case. Nonetheless, Gail remains confident and positive, thanks in large part to volunteer work.

"It's a terrific outlet for my creative energies," writes Gail, who chairs the public relations committee for the local branch of an important national charity organization. "I feel important, needed and worthwhile," she says. "I'm gaining new skills and knowledge. And I'm definitely connected to society — I just don't get paid for it."

Like most of us, Gail isn't entirely immune to negative feelings. "But when I work with that team of dedicated volunteers," she says, "I feel like such a winner."

Volunteer work not only keeps one's spirits up, it can be an important part of a job search, Gail believes.

"Who knows? Maybe a new person I meet will lead me to a job. Maybe a new skill I have learned will be important in the next position I apply for. Maybe my volunteer activities on my resume will differentiate me from the next candidate. Maybe my enthusiasm and confidence will burst forth the next time I talk about my volunteer work in an interview."

With similar enthusiasm, Ruth L. works tirelessly at her job search.

A couple of years ago, in an attempt to leave behind the troubled film industry, Ruth went back to school. She studied book and magazine publishing and today is looking for work in publishing.

"Some people would say that was stupid," Ruth writes. "The future jobs are in computer sciences and service areas. But if you hate these types of jobs, what's the point? You've got to do what you love. And I love words."

Ruth spends much of her time "networking," talking to people in the publishing world in search of advice, information and leads.

"You have to be alert at all times to follow up on clues, hints and job leads," Ruth writes. "You have to be thinking of angles to your job search continually, not just from 9 to 5."

One way to achieve this, she says, is to accept that some things you can control, and some you can't. For instance, Ruth has no control over "when and where jobs will show up, how an interviewer sees me, and the general state of the economy," she says. "What I can control are my reactions to these things."

Look to friends and relatives for support, Ruth suggests. "I've developed a small personal support network. They root for me, they empathize, they help me see the exit when I feel trapped. Some of them share their problems with me, which keeps me from becoming totally self-absorbed."

Somehow, we've all got to change the way we think, Ruth believes. "We can no longer define ourselves by a job title. What you do for a living is only part of who you are."

Last summer, to help a fellow student who felt suicidal, Ruth put together *Rules To Remember In The Search For A Job*. The list helped her friend get through a rough time, and Ruth offers it to others looking for work. It can be adapted to anyone's situation, she says.

> Accept that some things you can control, and some you can't.

1. **It's not my fault. I'm doing the best I can.**

2. **I'm allowed to make mistakes. I've never been taught the art/science of finding a job. At times, I'm going to stumble and fall.**

3. **I'm allowed to feel depressed. This is a difficult time, so jobs are harder to find than ever before. I must keep looking.**

4. **I'm allowed to feel sad. Rejection hurts.**

5. I am not alone.

6. If 80 per cent of jobs are never advertised, it will take some time to find one.

7. I'm allowed to take time out to do things that give me some pleasure. It's my reward for holding my head up and persevering.

8. I know what my skills are and I know I can do a good job. I am conscientious, responsible, creative, and strong. I am a valuable addition to anyone's project.

9. I must not be shy, afraid to impose. I'm looking for work and possible job leads. I can't do that without help. There is no shame in asking for help.

10. My handicaps are mostly imagined, and are not visible.

11. I may not have a job, but I'm still human.

12. I will not starve to death. Even if I hit a really tough patch, too many people love me to let that happen.

13. Success follows hard work. If I bang on enough doors, eventually one will open.

Believing you can

"My confidence is perilously shaky," a reader's letter confides. "Two months ago, I was let go. How do I adopt a positive attitude in light of this situation?"

It's not an easy question to answer. Maintaining a positive attitude during times of unemployment is a tricky proposition.

When you lose a job, even when you're worried that you might, dark clouds of uncertainty move into your neighborhood. Much of the time, they hover directly overhead. On good days, they disperse somewhat and lurk along the horizon. But they're always there, subtly eroding personal confidence.

As much as self-confidence is a job-search issue, it's equally important in career management. The point was clearly made in another letter from a different reader.

"I'm in my mid-30s," he writes. "Since I was very young I have faced the same chronic problem: a major lack of self-confidence.

"I hold a degree in mechanical engineering but I have never thought that I could be successful in my job. And I have never been. What do you think can be done?"

Positive thinking and a healthy self-image are bound up in each other. There's no easy route to either. There's no magic wand to dispel feelings of inadequacy and insecurity. And when such feelings dominate, positive thinking is a pointless exercise.

Some experts say we can change the way we view ourselves. It's also possible, even in uncertain times like these, to find and maintain a positive outlook. But neither can happen without strong commitment, a lot of hard work, and vigilant follow-up.

The course of our lives, both professional and personal, is predicated, in large part, on our self-image. It is our "personal blueprint for life," Maxwell Maltz wrote in his book *Psycho-cybernetics* (Simon and Schuster).

"All actions, feelings, behavior, even ... abilities are always consistent with this self-image," he argued.

Maltz, a plastic surgeon who saw the sometimes limited effect improved appearance had on his patient's feelings of inferiority, was among the first to examine "self-image psychology" in the early '60s.

> Positive thinking and a healthy self-image are bound up in each other.

Self-image, Maltz came to believe, is the key to personality and human behavior. It also sets the boundaries of individual accomplishment.

It is, in other words, an integral part of our being. Our self-image has "unconsciously been formed from our past experiences, our successes and failures, our humiliations, triumphs and the way other people have reacted to us, especially in early childhood," Maltz wrote.

To change or strengthen it, we have to re-program the internal tapes that govern our perceptions, not only of ourselves, but of the world at large. That's where the hard work comes in.

Although one of the first to write about self-image development, Maltz was not the last. There is now a large selection of books available on how to build confidence and self-esteem. Many provide insight and inspiration. A half hour spent in the psychology section of a large bookstore can give you a sense of what's available and what appeals.

Look for *Do What You Love, The Money Will Follow* (Dell Books). In it, author Marsha Sinetar relates self-esteem to career choices.

"High self-esteem provides the power to know what and who we are," Sinetar writes. "By contrast, those with low self-esteem do not know what they want out of life."

Building self-esteem and a satisfying life — work and otherwise — is not a single event but a lengthy process. Those embarking on this quest will need "a capacity to wait," Sinetar says, warning against "vainly wishing to be magically transformed."

Check your library for another book (currently out of print) written by psychotherapist Pauline R. Clance, *The Imposter Phenomenon, Overcoming The Fear That Haunts Your Success*. People often present a confident facade, a mask, Clance writes. Behind it, they're apprehensive, distressed and plagued by feelings of self-doubt. Her book looks at ways to take off the mask and keep it off.

If assertiveness is an issue, you might want to take a look at *Your Perfect Right, A Guide To Assertive Living* (Impact Publishers). Written by Robert Alberti and Michael Emmons, it reads like a textbook on assertiveness training.

TIP

"If an employer doesn't call you back, don't take it personally," says career specialist Barbara Simmons. "Keep in mind that filling a position is only a small portion of their work. Be proactive. Find a way to keep your name and interest known to them."

Chapter 6

PUTTING IT
ON THE LINE

BRIAN HUGHES

Resumes are highly personalized documents designed, much like brochures, to persuade people to call or write and ask for more information.

This is how Mark, a *Career Monitor* reader who recently moved to Ontario from British Columbia, handled his:

"I looked at every book I could get my hands on about resume writing and job hunting. After conducting this research, I decided a resume combining the characteristics of the functional and chronological resume formats was most suitable for me. I spent an intense week writing and reviewing the resume. I had it finished and polished before we moved."

Mark's approach is the right one. Creating a winning resume is intense work. Throughout the process, keep your audience — employers — in mind.

A great deal has been published about resumes. Before sitting down to write or assess yours, take a look at several of these publications.

Employers look for clues

"What do employers look for on a resume?"

The question is almost impossible to answer with any certainty. Employers are individuals and, like all of us, have subjective views on lots of topics, resumes included. What appeals to one doesn't necessarily appeal to another.

Career Monitor asked several employers and personnel specialists, many of whom recruit regularly: "What attracts you to one resume over another?" It wasn't a scientific sampling. Everyone surveyed admitted to having his or her own biases. Nonetheless, there does seem to be a consensus on the main points. If you're trying to write, or re-write, a resume that doesn't seem to be working for you, pay attention to the views of the people who do the hiring.

Resumes should be clear, concise and brief, they believe.

"Two pages — maximum; anything over that is getting too long," says David Peters, a human resources manager with Royal Trust.

"It doesn't matter how long you've been working. I don't really care, frankly, about the stuff you did in 1972. If you're in the 20th year of your career and you feel you must note it, make a brief chronological laundry list as an addendum," Peters adds.

Most of those surveyed agreed on another point: Don't bother to attach references to your resume. A simple notation at the end — *references available on request* — is adequate.

"Quality" is what Judith Kidd looks for when scanning resumes to decide whom to interview. "If there's a spelling mistake, it goes to the bottom," says Kidd, manager of human resources for McCarthy Tétrault, one of Canada's largest law firms. "If (the resume) is addressed to a particular individual, the name must be spelled correctly. It's the detail, and the care they've taken. If they don't care about that, are they going to care about our clients?"

One professional, who asked not to be identified, cautioned against using a resume that's "so slick it was obviously written by someone else." A recruiter for a major firm in the retail service sector, she had this to say: "There are a lot of professionally written resumes around right now. They make it practically impossible to conclude whether or not the person fits the job opening."

Resumes of this sort open with "one page of accomplishments or point-form notes that say: `I did this, or I did that,'" she says. "But they don't tell me about their work experience, or how long they worked at any particular place. You can tell by looking at it that the person who sent it didn't write it."

> "It's the detail, and the care they've taken. If they don't care about that, are they going to care about our clients?"

Above all, the information on a resume must be easily accessible to the reader, says David Peters. It's a simple factor of time. It's not unusual these days to "sit and go through two or three hundred resumes at a time," Peters says. "You can't afford to spend 10 minutes going over each resume. If you haven't told me in the first minute and a half what it is you do, I'm not going to bother looking for it."

The best resumes, Peters says, offer "a concise representation of a career in reverse chronological order."

Under each job "list major responsibilities and accomplishments in bullet, point-form rather than paragraph," he suggests. "A resume stands out if it has a lot of white space — almost like a good ad — with clearly blocked, easy-to-read, short sentences that give nothing but information."

And be sure, Peters adds, to "stay away from heavy adjectives and superfluous information."

Several of the people surveyed mentioned the importance of the covering letter. But no one put as much emphasis on it as Ira Travers, executive vice-president and general manager of Cal-Abco, a distributor for the micro-computer industry.

"I read a lot into the psychology of the letter," Travers says. "The resume tells me where they've been in the past. The covering letter tells me what kind of person they are."

Over all, what Travers looks for is "sincere comments."

"And I look for things that are tailored towards our industry. I want to interview people who've done some research and who can talk with some industry knowledge."

The message is clear. When employers review your resume and covering letter, even your application form, they're searching for clues. Not only about your skills and experience, but about your personality, your attitude and your work habits.

"You can find out levels of sincerity, levels of sensitivity and how concerned people are about doing the job you want them to do," Travers explains.

"If it's a form letter, I generally don't even bother to read the rest of the application."

TIP

When filling out an application form, it can be difficult to know how to handle the salary question — both salary expected and previous salary, says career and human resource consultant Sandy Wise, "particularly if your previous salary was high and you know you're not going to duplicate that.

"Don't leave it blank," Wise says. "It looks like you've forgotten. If you are flexible, put in the word 'negotiable' for salary expected."

When asked about your previous salary, "put in a range, say $10 to $16 (an hour)," Wise suggests. "It shows that you started low and worked up. It also indicates that you might be willing to do that again."

Take a close look at your resume

"It's so frustrating. I've never been out of work this long before. I'm starting to wonder about myself. I'm starting to wonder if there's something I'm doing wrong."

Sound familiar? No doubt you've had similar thoughts yourself if you're among the people who can't find work at the moment. Never mind that the statistics say thousands upon thousands are in the same boat. Never mind that, in some fields especially, there are simply no jobs available. When months drag by, and nothing happens, the average individual is likely to take it personally.

Quite possibly, there's little more you can do. Like many people today, you're caught in a waiting game. If you keep doing what you're doing and don't lose heart, you're going to find work.

Then again, maybe your approach to job hunting isn't all that effective, or part of it isn't. If something isn't working, it's up to you to change it.

Either way, after months of job search, a critical and objective review of how you're looking for work is a smart move. A fresh look at your approach and the obstacles that seem to be in your way may help you come up with creative ways to overcome them.

Look first at your written work, at the resumes and letters you send prospective employers. If they're not opening doors for you, perhaps they're closing them.

> A resume can't get you a job. What it's meant to do is generate interest and interviews.

A resume can't get you a job. What it's meant to do is generate interest and interviews. If it's not doing that, if it's not producing close to a 10 per cent return on effort — 100 resumes sent, 10 indications of interest — it may need some work.

Take a hard look at it. Be brutally objective. What does it say about you? Does it feature your strengths? Does it catch the reader's attention early and encourage one to read on? Most of all, does it give the reader any reason to screen you out?

Earl, a salesman, and a good one at that, has been out of work for months now. At 53, his age and the fact that he doesn't have a college education work against him in the job market, he believes.

Yet, on the top of the first page, a key spot in any resume — because it's there you either catch someone's interest or begin to lose it — Earl has an *EDUCATION* section, noting his high school diploma and the year he received it.

So, up front, long before reading about his impressive work history and accomplishments, an employer can easily figure out what Earl would prefer not to emphasize — how old he is and that he didn't go to university.

It's not unusual for job candidates to provide too much detail on their resumes, according to one survey of 200 executive employers. They also frequently miss typing mistakes and grammatical errors, and fail to consider whether the document has a professional appearance, the executives said.

Even worse than that, these employers suspect that more than a quarter of all job applicants lie, or intentionally omit information on their resumes.

Finding the middle ground between saying too much on a resume or not enough can take some effort, says Paul McDonald, president of the recruiting firm Robert Half/Accountemps, which conducted the survey. Job seekers who qualify for more than one type of job should have more than one resume, McDonald suggests. Each one should be truthful, but emphasize different aspects of experience.

The most impressive resumes, he says, echoing the feelings of many employers, are "factual but brief, sticking to relevant job-related information. They have wide margins and plenty of space between paragraphs."

Employers also want to hear about your achievements on a resume, the survey found.

At the same time, some information should never appear on a resume, according to McDonald. Never indicate past salaries, he says, or reason for termination, names of references or past supervisors, political, fraternal or religious affiliations, race, national origin, sex, or personal characteristics.

Don't date your resume either, and never include a photograph, he adds.

A careful review of your resume against McDonald's list of *shoulds* and *shouldn'ts* may indicate a need for revisions. If so, take time to do them thoroughly. And once you've re-worked it, take it to three people in your field whose opinion you respect and ask them to critique it.

Don't become defensive when they make comments. Keep an open mind. Listen carefully and take notes. Incorporate any valid suggestions in your final draft.

You'll want to do a similar review of the letters you send to employers. Read them objectively. Are they personalized and tailored to each job and each employer? If not, they'll never stand out from the hundreds of others that compete for an employer's attention these days.

When a manager has been laid off due to the cancellation of a project, how should this information be presented on a resume?

Janis Foord Kirk
Career Monitor

AND IN REPLY

It's not necessary to put a reason for leaving on a resume. In fact, it is not advisable. If you feel you'd like to explain the circumstances in your written application, do so in a covering letter. If the cancellation of the project was outside your control, find a way to make that clear.

Chapter 7

BE KIND TO
YOUR REFEREES

SUSAN TODD

References can be crucial

I f you're looking for work, some time in the not too distant future people you don't know will be calling people with whom you used to work to ask questions about you.

They'll be checking references, trying to assess whether the things you've told them about yourself are accurate, trying to assess whether you "fit" the job they're trying to fill.

Although you're the reason for the call and the topic of conversation, you'll no doubt feel that you have little control over what's said.

But in fact, as a job seeker you *can* play a role in the reference-checking process. If you're prepared to be honest and discuss your circumstances objectively, you can exert some influence over what's said in a reference enquiry.

> "Never burn bridges. Keep in contact. Let them know whenever you give their names out."

Employers and recruiters use a variety of techniques to decide whether you're suited to a particular job. They assess your resume, your performance in interviews, occasionally they give you psychological tests.

And, they check references.

Reference checking is "not perfect, not failproof," says Tom Sinclair, a search consultant with Coopers & Lybrand Consulting Group. "But it's a very important assessment tool."

So important, Sinclair says, that in 1990 he organized and sponsored, together with the legal firm Borden & Elliot, a seminar on the topic for about a hundred Canadian companies.

A poll of the people at that gathering, human resource and personnel professionals, reveals the strong emphasis employers place on reference enquiries.

Ninety-nine per cent said they checked references, most before offering a job. According to these professionals, written references were of minimal value. Eighty-four per cent of their reference enquiries were made verbally, over the phone, they said.

When handled thoroughly, reference questions cover technical abilities, education, practical experience and responsibilities, reason for leaving, salary, job performance and personal characteristics, says Sinclair.

Employers and recruiters telephone your "referees," as they are called, to confirm what you told them in the interview, as well as to check out any hunches they may have about you. From there, the questioning will move into any "areas of concern" about a job applicant's ability to handle the job in question.

"Say the person has been late for every meeting with you and tardiness would be a real problem in the job. You look for details on their punctuality," Sinclair explains.

Calls like these make people feel exposed. Few of us are fully confident about what others think of us and our work. Working behind the scenes to influence what will be said can help to relieve the uncertainty.

The first reference that people want is someone who has supervised you. This reference can be difficult to offer if you're working and looking for a new job at the same time.

"Line up a list of names and numbers," Sinclair suggests. On this list include people you used to work with, people who've recently left your organization, or anyone within the organization who knows of your plans and who you feel you can trust. (Be cautious about the latter, he advises.)

Keep these people informed. Make sure they see your resume. Go over it with them and keep in contact. Let them know whenever you give their names out, so they'll be prepared.

If you've been laid-off or fired, you'll no doubt feel especially vulnerable knowing reference calls are being made to the people who recently rejected you.

Even here, though, planning and forethought can pay dividends.

First and foremost, "never burn bridges," Sinclair advises. If you're fired, try to curb your anger. "Don't go into the president's office, take a strip off his back and then expect the company to say glowing things about you a couple of weeks down the road."

And always be totally open and honest with prospective employers. Be objective and don't embellish the facts. The information you pass on in interviews can come back to haunt you.

If what you say differs significantly from the information provided by a referee, for example, your credibility goes out the window.

"Don't make up a story about why you left," Sinclair says. "If you know it was a performance issue, be open and honest.

"If you were let go and you suspect there was more to it than you were told, when you talk to a prospective employer preface your reason for leaving with `this is what I was told.'"

And talk to your ex-boss, Sinclair suggests. "Try to sort out what will be said and what won't be said."

Employment lawyer Randall Echlin, a partner with Borden & Elliot, puts it this way:

"Spend time thinking about references and structuring them. Decide who you're going to give by way of references. Invest the time going through with them what you see as being your strengths and weaknesses. Develop with them what you're going to tell prospective employers as to the reason why you parted company."

Work to be objective, Echlin says. "You have to be able to say, `I'm strong in this, and weak in that and that's why I'm changing jobs. My last job wasn't right for me; it was a mis-match of my skills. It didn't work out, but that doesn't mean I can't do a whiz-bang job for you.'"

T I P

"Send a copy of your resume along with a thank-you letter to everyone who has agreed to act as a reference," suggests career specialist Barbara Simmons. "This will update their information about you and the skills you've acquired since they last had contact with you. As well, they'll be able to speak more eloquently about you when they receive calls."

Foot-dragging can hurt

"One time, it took my old boss two weeks to get back to the recruiter," June says. "The position I was being considered for went to someone else.

"Another time, they didn't talk to my boss but someone in human resources," she continues. "It wasn't necessarily a negative review but more 'Yes, she was here. Now she's gone and who cares.' I didn't get that job, either."

Few job-search concerns are fraught with as much uncertainty and as many misconceptions as what employers say about you after you're gone.

Most of the uncertainty occurs on the part of people like June who need a positive review. Since she was fired a year and a half ago, she's made many more than 1,000 job applications. She's had about 10 interviews, she says, but nothing has come of them. As the months go by, the question, "what are they saying about me?" takes on new meaning.

Her actual firing wasn't handled well or sensitively, June says. Those reference enquiries haven't been, either.

This is more common than not. In the 1990 survey mentioned earlier, only about a quarter of the 100 Canadian companies polled had a formal policy in place regarding references.

When no company policy exists, staff members outside the personnel department are given little if any training or instruction on how to handle reference enquiries as they come up. Supervisors, peers and subordinates often don't know how to respond to questions.

This ad hoc approach makes job seekers like June nervous.

"Today, even a hint of negativity is suicide," she explains. "And people have the audacity to assume that they can interpret 'ums' and 'ahs' from your reference as being negative. The result is no interview or, if an interview has already occurred, no offer."

June's concerns are justified, given the importance most employers attach to references.

If anything, they have become even more important in recent years, says Coopers & Lybrand's Tom Sinclair.

"In a slower economy, we find the hiring process slows down," he explains. "People want to be more and more sure that they've got the right candidate. We're asked to do more references, and at an earlier stage (of the recruiting process) than in the past."

> Each link in the chain must be strong if the reference process is to work.

There are three links in the reference chain — the past employer, the prospective employer and, in the middle, the hopeful employee. Each link must be strong if the reference process is to work and help the employee land a new job.

In June's case, her previous employer is the weak link.

When her company "reorganized," June's counterpart in another division was given her responsibilities. "My then-supervisor informed me that the reason for my dismissal had no bearing on me or my performance," she says.

However, that supervisor now evades calls or passes them on to the human resources department. The human resources department has adopted what employment lawyer Randall Echlin describes as the "name, rank and serial number" response.

By limiting comments in this way, companies do former employees a disservice, says Echlin, of Borden & Elliot. "It sends a negative message when you don't intend to. And there's no real risk to employers when they give a full reference."

Still, according to the 1990 survey, prospective employers find it increasingly difficult to get references.

People sometimes resist giving out information about past employees because of a "fear of the unknown," Echlin says. "They've heard about defamation. They're afraid to say something negative, so they'd rather say nothing and hope that gets their head out of the noose."

In fact, there is little for employers to fear, says Echlin.

"Be candid," he advises. "Be open. Be honest. Don't be afraid of bogeymen. There are none. If a reference is honestly given, without malice, the defence is there in defamation law."

In fact, Echlin says, "the law views candid references as being essential in commercial practices."

Both Echlin and Sinclair suggest that the reference discussion focus on the individual's talents, strengths and "job fit." At the same time, they say, referees should be willing to discuss shortcomings, as well.

Being prepared to discuss a past employee openly and honestly takes some planning. Still, it's to everyone's advantage to ensure that any organization considering hiring a new employee has access to an objective view of his or her past work.

Chapter 8

TECHNOLOGY, ORGANIZATION AND JOB-SEARCH ETIQUETTE

THOMAS DANNENBERG

Breaking through the electronic barriers

Applying for work has taken on new meaning in this electronic age. More often than not nowadays, long before they see the whites of your eyes, employers receive an electronic message from you. Maybe you fax your resume. Or you introduce yourself on electronic telephone-answering equipment. In a few cases — extremely rare to date — they may even see your life and times featured on video.

First impressions can be lasting impressions. Electronic communication, impersonal and distant though it may seem, gives employers a basis on which to make judgments about you, and about your ability to do the job.

Presenting yourself professionally through this sometimes bewildering array of equipment and technology is a necessary job-hunting skill in the '90s. And it can take some effort to make certain that the message sent on it — or *to* it — does the trick, and gets you that face-to-face meeting.

> "Remember that a faxed resume comes out black and white on nasty paper."

Over a couple of weeks, Elizabeth LaFontaine met nearly 200 job seekers — electronically speaking. Few of their electronic presentations made her want to meet them in person.

LaFontaine owns and manages a communications and special-events company, which she runs from her home. The company is 15 months old and growing, she says.

In search of administrative help, LaFontaine ran a classified help-wanted ad. Small and a single column wide, it appeared for only one day. Qualified people were asked to fax resumes, or to reply to a special telephone number.

One hundred and seventy-five people responded and LaFontaine was "quite literally overwhelmed," she says.

What became obvious as she began to analyze the resumes and phone calls, however, was that few of those who applied had given much thought to how their application would appear to the person receiving it.

"I think people don't realize that somebody who puts an ad in the paper these days will likely get hundreds of replies," LaFontaine observes. "Unless an application jumps up and down and hits you in the face, it might not even get read."

Be extremely careful about layout and design, she suggests. Remember that a faxed resume "comes out black and white on nasty paper."

"With a little bit of imagination, you can make it more interesting," LaFontaine says. "One I remember had a border and was well laid-out. Quite honestly, I got to the stage where I looked at those that really looked nice."

Be sure, as well, to target your audience. Many of the people who sent a resume to LaFontaine "simply flung it into the fax machine without thinking it needed a covering letter," she says. Had they been mailing them, she suspects, they'd have added a letter describing how their background met the requirements of the job.

Finally, LaFontaine believes, 90 per cent of resumes are too long and provide too much detail. One she received ran to 13 pages and made her almost angry. "Such a waste of paper," she says.

Among the most requested job skills these days — in all kinds of industries and for all sorts of positions — is the ability to communicate clearly and succinctly. Your resume and letter indicate your skill with the written word. Spoken communication skills are evident every time you call someone, or leave a message on an answering machine.

If you're articulate and think quickly, you no doubt have little trouble with telephone answering equipment. A great many people, however, need to work to overcome communication barriers. In part, this means anticipating the needs of the person who gets your message.

The majority of people who called LaFontaine, for example, left only their name and number. In doing so, they missed an opportunity to sell her on calling them back.

"When you get so many messages, it's impossible to get back to everyone," she says. "I couldn't get enough information to know who to call back.

"It's not fair, I know, but you pre-judge people by their voice and what they say," adds LaFontaine, who suggests job applicants write a script and practise a bit before calling an answering machine. In a job market like ours, the telephone-answering machine ceases to be a message service and becomes instead a screening tool.

The screening of job applicants using telephone technology took a leap forward with the introduction by the Toronto Star of a "voice resume" service. Employers placing job ads can now rent this service. When they do, special phone numbers are noted in their ads.

If the job described in an ad seems suited to you, you call the number and a taped message asks specific questions — up to 10 of them. Once you've answered them, your replies automatically play back, allowing you to hear how they sound.

If you're not pleased with your verbal presentation, you cancel the file by hanging up. This then becomes a practice run, and you call again. Once you are happy with your answers, you "file" the voice resume by punching certain numbers on your phone.

You're then given a code and asked to call back in 48 hours. The employer reviews your answers, and leaves a message for you, saying either send a resume, call for an interview, or "thanks but no thanks."

At the high-end executive level, we're seeing the emergence of video resumes designed to provide employers with a first-hand, documentary view of executives on the job and at play. Production of video resumes starts at about $3,000.

Technology of this sort has added another chapter to the book on job-search etiquette. Anticipating the needs of the employer at the other end of an electronic communication can give you an edge.

T I P

"Use a tape recorder to assess how you sound in an interview, or on voice mail or an answering machine," suggests career management specialist Loretta Helman. "Prepare a two-minute presentation of your work experience, special skills and areas of strength."

Using your computer to get organized

The best way to get over losing a job is to find another. And the best way to go about finding one is to wage an organized and proactive job search — like Michael S. did.

Some time ago, Michael lost his job as director of materials for a manufacturing company in the aerospace industry. He was one of seven managers to be let go when his employer "restructured," he says.

Since then, with his home office as action central, Michael has been conducting a systematic and professional job search. He wrote *Career Monitor* to share some of the techniques he's developed for job hunting in what he calls "our very difficult market."

Before most potential employers meet Michael, they read his work. Early in his job search, he took care to ensure the quality of this written presentation. "I had my resume screened and critiqued by other professionals, by former bosses and by friends," he writes. "The format is clear and easy to read, listing education, career history, and accomplishments.

"After I became unemployed, I purchased a letter-quality printer," he adds. "It was well justified. I print a master copy of my resume for photocopying and each introduction letter is tailored to the company to which it is being sent.

"I have a basic letter in the computer," Michael explains. "Say, I'm writing to a firm that makes heat exchangers for the automobile industry. I'm able to address the letter to a specific person and insert a paragraph telling them I know of them and the work they do."

Michael operates a personal computer with proficiency, thanks, he says, to a Grade 9 typing class and a week-long Lotus 1-2-3 course that he took four years ago. Computer technology isn't essential to a professional job search, he says, but it helps.

It keeps him organized. "I keep a perpetual diary of my job search on a Symphony (an advanced version of Lotus 1-2-3) spreadsheet," he writes. "It lists the firm, the location, and the date the resume was mailed.

"Every time I get a response, I document it," Michael says. "There's a column for the date of the response (if any) and the type of response ('no requirement at this time,' etc)."

Michael's software allows him to sort the spreadsheet in various ways — "by sector, location and, of course, by date. I use the date sort to 'age' how long a resume has been out to any particular firm."

Over a three-month period, Michael used this system to make about 300 job applications. Nearly 100 were based on leads from people in his network of "previous employers and colleagues." The remainder — more than 150, Michael figures — have been made to companies listed in *Business Connexions*, a directory of about 200,000 Canadian companies. He also responded to 30 or so job advertisements.

The directory, which categorizes companies alphabetically as well as by industry and province, "saves me many trips to the Chamber of Commerce or the library," Michael writes. He's into it daily, he says, looking for companies in the aerospace industry as well as other manufacturers "with different product lines."

Business Connexions lists the company's name, address, and phone and fax numbers. Because Michael came to accept the wisdom of contacting the person who would be his boss instead of the human resources department, he now phones to get the name of the president or vice-president of operations before writing. "Ninety-five per cent of the time I get the name, no problem," he says.

Of the people Michael writes to, fewer than a third respond. Nonetheless, he's had three job interviews and another "there's-nothing-at-the-moment-but-let's-talk" meeting. Two possibilities are still active, he says.

If there's a weakness in his job-search technique, it's that he doesn't follow up with those firms that don't respond to his application. The number of job interviews generated by a mail campaign like this has been known to double with the addition of a follow-up telephone call.

Michael has no illusions about the difficulties he has yet to face in the job market. "It's scary out there," he acknowledges. "But I keep optimistic. I still get up at the regular time every morning. I get the papers, scan them, then spend time going through the directory. Every day, I make at least one application.

"It does get frustrating at times," he admits. "But I go for long walks and have talks with myself about being positive."

Staying positive, keeping organized, following up on leads — there are as many different combinations of these essentials as there are job seekers. Michael's systematized approach is a worthy model.

Chapter 9

HANDLING INTERVIEWS

ANDREW SKUJA

Careful planning puts you in charge

I t's mid-afternoon, Tuesday. You're at the kitchen table, trying to put the finishing touches on a covering letter you want to get in the mail by 5. The job you're applying for was advertised in the weekend paper. It sounds exactly like the sort of thing you've been looking for.

For most of the afternoon, you've been plunking away at your typewriter, your frustration growing. It's important to hit the right note in this letter and this is your third attempt. It still doesn't feel right.

The phone rings. You answer curtly, preoccupied with your task and a little annoyed at being interrupted.

"This is the personnel manager at Permanent Pavement. We received your resume last week. We're looking for an administrator for our regional office. Do you have a few moments?"

As you push your letter aside to talk, whether you realize it or not, you've agreed to a telephone screening interview.

Job interviews are conversations between you and one or more people about your suitability for a particular position. They come in all shapes and sizes.

> "You can get a job without a resume, but you can't get a job without an interview."

You can be interviewed in a 10-minute phone call, or leaning up against a counter in a personnel office. More often, though, you'll be interviewed in an office, behind closed doors. Interviews generally take 30 minutes to an hour. However, some go on for several hours, and others take place over an entire day.

When looking for work, you can't escape the interview process. As authors Kathryn and Ross Petras say in *The Only Job Hunting Guide You'll Ever Need* (Poseidon Press): "You can get a job without a resume, but you can't get a job without an interview."

"Recognize what an interview is and what it isn't," they suggest. "It is not a rehashing of your resume, nor is it merely an opportunity to answer questions an interviewer may pose; interviewing is salesmanship. It is selectively presenting the facts in an organized, confident manner so that you can sell yourself into a job."

It's good advice. Most job seekers work hard at it. What's especially frustrating about interviews, however, is that they're often highly subjective. When the "chemistry" works, you know it. When it doesn't, that's obvious as well.

Still, if you know what to expect, if you prepare well and keep your wits about you, it's possible, at least to some degree, to generate positive chemistry in conversations like these.

Say a sensitive question like, "Why did you leave your last job?" comes to you over the phone in the middle of a frustrating afternoon of letter writing. You're not likely to handle it well.

Employers conduct telephone screening interviews to get additional information before deciding whether to set up a meeting. Rather than automatically agreeing to a telephone interview, if you're busy, or preoccupied, or if you don't feel prepared, ask to return the call. Jumping in unprepared could actually get you screened out.

Recruiters and personnel agency consultants and human resource staff also conduct screening interviews face to face. In these instances, interviewers are not looking for just one suitable candidate, but several. They're developing a short list of people who can potentially do the job. They'll refer several people to the line-manager for an actual employment interview.

Employment interviews with line managers tend to be highly specific. Stay away from generalities. Provide a clear sense of your performance on the job. You now have a captive audience — the person who would supervise your work. This is not only the ultimate decision maker, it's the person with the best understanding of the job and the team of people with whom you would work. Be ready to articulate, very clearly, what excites you about the position.

Hiring decisions in the public sector and in large institutions are often made on the basis of panel or group interviews. Interviews of this sort will be discussed in depth later in this chapter.

After a successful screening interview, some large organizations bring people in for an all-day interview. During the course of that day, job applicants can meet up to eight people. The challenge here, as in all lengthy interviews, is to continue to sound spontaneous.

Kathryn and Ross Petras write: "Interviewers often turn down applicants who sound overly rehearsed with their presentations: this was frequently mentioned as the biggest turnoff by interviewers at a large packaged-goods corporation."

In highly structured interviews there will be a strict agenda for your meeting. These interviews usually are conducted by personnel officers in large organizations.

"This requires every candidate to answer the same questions in the same order," suggest Robert Wegmann and Robert Chapman in *The Right Place At The Right Time* (Ten Speed Press). "When you run into one of these, just sit back and answer the questions."

Structured interviews are probably the only ones in which simply sitting back and answering questions is advisable. Generally, the more questions you ask, the more involved you are in the interview, the more positive it's likely to be.

No matter what style of interview you find yourself in, keep in mind that there are two different agendas. Interviewers represent employers. Their role is to question, and probe, and to assess your suitability for the job. You, as a job seeker, have a couple of goals — to discuss your background and skills and how they relate to the job in question and to find out all you can about the position, the department, the company.

Prepare thoroughly

> The objective of research is to put together a profile of the hiring organization.

Preparing for an interview is a lot like preparing for a sales presentation. You learn everything you can about the circumstances and needs of your customer (the employer). You assess the various features of your product (that's you). You work to find the most direct way to tell people how your product can fulfil their needs (your presentation).

It's a subtle process that requires your close attention on several levels.

First, there's appearance. Like it or not, the way you look leaves an impression on others. Be objective and assess your image. How appropriate is it for the job you're going after?

Next, examine your information base and do what you can to bring it up to date. "Learn about the company, the position, and if possible, the interviewer as well," advise Kathryn and Ross Petras.

"Read annual reports, trade magazines, and company literature.... Always be on the lookout for information you can use to make yourself sound more knowledgeable, more interested, and better than the other applicants."

The person (or people) you'll meet in an interview represent an organization with very specific needs and concerns. It will be easier to relate to them — and impress them — if you have an understanding of their products and services, corporate culture, reputation and competitors. Look also for information on industry advances and common problems throughout the industry as a whole.

The objective of this research is to put together a profile of the hiring organization. Once you have it, look for ways your background and experience fit that profile. Here's an example of how this can work from the Petras' book, *The Only Job Hunting Guide You'll Ever Need*:

"Should a company's literature make reference to an entrepreneurial corporate culture and their need for self-starting employees, start thinking before the interview of items to mention that will highlight your own entrepreneurial past."

The dynamics of each interview will differ, depending on things such as conversational style, the motives of the interviewer, the training he or she has — or hasn't — had, and the chemistry between you and the people you meet. Interviews may be highly structured, or they may be casual and unfocused. Some interviewers will be pleasant and encouraging, others distant and judgmental. Some will even be confrontational.

Thomas is a recruiter for a large consulting firm. He has a direct, no-nonsense, sometimes confrontational style. He asks pointed questions. When he senses a weakness, he probes around it relentlessly. Job applicants have been known to collapse in relief against his office door as it closes behind them.

"I recruit sales people," Thomas explains. "They have to be able to take the heat."

The message is clear. In an interview, you have to be ready to adapt, no matter what they throw at you.

TIP

"Approach interviews as if you were on a research mission rather than a job interview," suggests career management specialist Loretta Helman. "Tell yourself: 'I'm looking for the ideal employer. I want to know about them as much as they want to know about me.' Ask them questions like: What are your needs in light of the current economy? What skills do you need now? What do you expect from your staff?"

Consider your answers— and questions

As we've already noted, in any job interview there are two distinct agendas. Interviewers represent the employer and want to learn about you: Do you have the skills and experience to do the job? Do you have the motivation and commitment they deem necessary? Will your personality and style fit the team that's already in place?

On the opposite side of the desk there's you, wanting to learn about the job: Does it fit your abilities? Will it challenge you, and for how long? What sort of people will you be working with? Are there future opportunities?

In an attempt to fulfil their agenda, interviewers ask questions. It's impossible to predict exactly what questions, but here are a few that are often asked and some of the motives behind them:

> **Prepare to discuss your strengths as they relate to the job in question.**

"Tell me about yourself."

Most job seekers hate this question. It's too open-ended, they say, too vague. Still, it's often the opening gambit in many interviews. What the interviewer is really saying is: "Tell me about yourself *in relation to this job*." If you're ready for it, the question provides an opportunity to begin your sales pitch.

"Avoid launching into a life history," advise Kathryn and Ross Petras in *The Only Job Hunting Guide You'll Ever Need.*

"Instead, give only the information that supports your credentials for the job. Briefly outline your background: past job history, goals, schooling, even hobbies or memberships, always relating them to the position you're interviewing for."

"What are your strengths?"

Answering this question directly isn't bragging, it's salesmanship. Prepare to discuss your strengths as they relate to the job in question. If you know it's a high-pressure job and you've got nerves of steel, say so. If the position needs a strong communicator, talk about your ability to express yourself clearly and draw people out. Give examples from your work history.

"What are your weaknesses?"

This is another common interview question. Some see it as a trick question, others say it's a stupid one. Nonetheless, answering it satisfactorily requires forethought.

Because most of an interview focuses on what you are and what you're capable of, this question is designed to provide some insight into what you aren't. Interviewers are looking for personal objectivity.

Kathryn and Ross Petras suggest that you never give a canned response that sounds rehearsed. "Whatever weakness you bring up, briefly stress how you've taken steps to overcome it," they write. "Self-improvement shows that you can not only see a flaw, you can act on it."

> **"Self-improvement shows that you can not only see a flaw, you can act on it."**

"Why did you leave your last employer?"

Those seeking greater challenge and responsibility who left a job (or plan to leave) on good terms probably will have little trouble with this question.

But perhaps you were let go, or nudged out in some way. Maybe you're harboring resentment. If so, this can be a touchy issue. At all costs, avoid bad-mouthing your employer — no matter how sympathetic the interviewer may seem.

Work diligently to develop a philosophical view of the circumstances. Something like: "Leaving wasn't my idea but it became necessary because.... Still, I learned a great deal in that job. Now I'm very keen to apply that knowledge to another position, like this one, that better suits my abilities." Then change the subject subtly by asking a pertinent question about the job.

"Why should we hire you?"

Expect a question of this sort toward the end of an interview. It may be worded in softer language, such as: "Are you interested in this job?"

This is another chance, and often your final chance, to sell yourself. Heed this advice from *The Only Job Hunting Guide You'll Ever Need*: "Explain why this is a logical position for you; sum up your work history and re-emphasize your strongest qualities and achievements ... let the interviewer know that you will be an asset to the company."

Throughout the interview, be prepared, as well, to field questions about your previous educational and employment choices, about your goals, your salary history and your current requirements.

And, although they're likely to come in oblique ways, expect some questions about your personal circumstances.

With each question asked, the interviewer ticks off an item on his or her agenda. Your role is to provide enough information to successfully complete that process, and at the same time, see that your own agenda is met.

"Start asking questions (of your own)," Wegmann and Chapman suggest. "It will take effort because the natural psychology of the interview leads you to sit back and answer the interviewer's questions.... Resist that inclination."

Be sure, though, that your questions are carefully considered.

"Don't ask just anything," they write. "Ask in as many ways as you can phrase it, one basic question: *'Just what is it you, the employer, want done?'*"

Here are some of the questions Wegmann and Chapman suggest you use to probe for information:

> "The art of interviewing lies in being ready to talk about your skills and accomplishments."

- "It would help me understand what you're looking for if I knew how you see the demands of the job."
- "Are there any aspects of the job you think need particular attention?"
- "What is the key skill or attitude that makes the difference in this position?"
- "If you hire exactly the person you want for this job, what will that person do for you in the first year on the job?"

Questions like these will help you develop a clear understanding of the job. Then target the conversation to your suitability for it.

"The art of interviewing," write Chapman and Wegmann, "lies in being ready to talk about your skills and accomplishments and in being able to adapt your presentation on the spot to what you have just learned about a particular position."

I lost my job due to bad relations with my supervisor. It happened after six years of co-operation. It was not exactly my fault and I don't feel guilty about it. Bosses have the right to fire subordinates, not vice versa.

In interviews, how can I answer the question, Why am I no longer with the last company?

Janis Foord Kirk
Career Monitor

AND IN REPLY

Your positive attitude shines through in your letter and I expect it will in interviews as well. An objective, dispassionate explanation of what happened, including a brief overview of the role you played and the lessons you learned, should be adequate.

Prepare well for interviews. Write down all your thoughts on the subject, then edit them to be certain they're clear and concise. Next, get a friend to ask you the question: "Why did you leave?"

Practise until you're comfortable discussing your departure.

New techniques probe your past

Whatever level they're being considered for — executive, managerial, support staff or blue collar — people find job interviews difficult.

It's not easy to convey a clear sense of your background and suitability for a specific job to someone you've never met before. Unless, that is, you're interviewed by someone so well versed in interview techniques that you have no choice.

Imagine, for a moment, that you answered an advertisement about a month ago for a job that sounds perfect for you. It took a while, but the company called last week to arrange an interview.

Today's the day.

The interview begins with questions about your knowledge and expertise. You're comfortable with these. You know you have the right background and training for the job.

Then the interviewer says: "I'd like to concentrate for a moment on how you organize your work. What skills do you use to manage your time?"

This one catches you napping. But you do have time management skills and you find a way to describe them.

The next question is more specific: "Tell me about a time when setting goals helped you complete a program on schedule."

And, a short while later: "Tell me about one of your projects that fell seriously behind schedule."

You thought you'd prepared well for this interview, but you aren't ready for this. You find yourself floundering.

The interviewer, sensing your discomfort, smiles encouragingly and begins to probe: "What was the project? What major obstacles did you encounter? How did you attempt to overcome those obstacles?"

You're in the midst of a "behavior description" interview.

It's a new style of interview, and though not that common yet, one day soon you might well find yourself faced with one.

Hiring mistakes are costly — some experts suggest they cost a company about half the yearly salary of the person who needs to be replaced. And studies have found behavior description (BD) interviewing to be one of the most accurate ways to assess future performance on the job.

So says Tom Janz, who, along with Lowell Hellervik and David Gilmore, pioneered the concept in the early '80s and co-wrote a book on the subject called *Behavior Description Interviewing* (distributed in Canada by Prentice Hall).

Janz, who holds a PhD in industrial organizational psychology, teaches at the University of Calgary. He also markets behavioral science technology.

According to Janz, a BD interview can predict future job performance more accurately than "traditional interviews, panel interviews, reference checks, cognitive ability tests and assessment centres. It has the highest accuracy in the published literature at this time," he says.

In their book, Janz and his colleagues explain the concept. "The best predictor of behavior in the future is behavior in the past," they write.

People trained to conduct BD interviews look for a story — or, as the authors describe it, a "critical incident" — from their past that will illustrate their skills and abilities in a specific situation. Interviewers are trained to probe, sometimes relentlessly, always kindly, for the information they want.

Recruiting staff at the Royal Bank of Canada has been using BD interviews for more than a year to recruit customer service representatives. Roy Samson, manager of recruitment and employment equity for one of the bank's larger districts, says that turnover in that area has decreased. He's careful to point out, however, that other factors — the economy, for instance — have influenced turnover as well. "People don't change jobs in a recession," he observes.

> "The best predictor of behavior in the future is behavior in the past."

Still, the BD style of interviewing provides "relevant, job-specific information," Samson says. "We ask questions directly related to past circumstances and how a person behaved in those circumstances.

"For instance, I might say: `Tell me about the last time you dealt with a customer who was unhappy with a service or product they'd been sold.' And the person would say: `Boy, that happens all the time.'

"Then, I'd say: 'What I'd like you to do is recall the best example of that, something that stands out in your mind.'

"And they'd say: 'Well, that happened a couple of weeks ago....' and then recite the story. It's almost like they're replaying a video of their life. It's very pertinent, real information which gives a complete and accurate picture of an individual's behavior."

Though the likelihood of encountering a BD interview is still fairly small, be prepared to tell stories about your past to illustrate your abilities on the job. It's the kind of advance planning that will pay off in an interview, whether you're asked behavior questions or not.

Story-telling can set you apart

"A picture paints a thousand words."

A cliché, yes. But, the truism at the root of it can be used to your advantage in job interviews.

No, you don't have to lug your photo album around. But you do have to work to find a way to paint pictures with your words. By telling work-related stories or vignettes you can give employers a true sense of how you perform on the job.

Here's how one sales professional, who worked in the bottling industry, used this technique to persuade an interviewer that he was the "creative salesperson" he'd claimed to be on his resume:

"Do you remember when the cooler craze first hit the beverage industry?" he began. "Well, it hit the States before Canada. I read an article in an industry trade magazine about how the trend had caught on and how significant it appeared to be. It was very factual, citing statistics of current and projected use.

"I got out to see my small bottling accounts right away. I gave them a copy of the article. Some of them got excited about it and I worked with them to help them prepare.

"The demand hit here about six months later. Quite a few of my customers were tooled up and ready to take advantage of it."

Stories like these have staying power. Long after the words, "I'm a creative sales representative" are forgotten, this vignette will remain, speaking volumes about the person who told it.

Some people are natural raconteurs and adopt this "storytelling" approach almost effortlessly. Many of us are less articulate, however, and prone to rambling accounts or to getting lost along verbal tangents. (You'll know you're in this category if people glaze over as you speak, or if you're often encouraged to "get to the point.")

A while ago, a colleague passed on a storytelling approach, called *situation/action/benefit*, that goes a long way toward overcoming this tendency to ramble. The formula goes like this:

You accept at the outset that the listener has no knowledge of the story you're about to tell, and set the stage by describing the situation fully.

Then you describe the action you took, taking full ownership of it.

You have to use the "I" word. Too often, not wanting to appear immodest, people relate past experiences using the corporate "we" instead. This is a mistake. It weakens the impact of the tale, making it sound like a team action rather than a personal one.

The punch line is the benefit of the action you took, or the satisfying conclusion to the story.

Finding situation/action/benefit stories to illustrate your skills and abilities takes forethought, planning and even some practice.

Say, you have an interview coming up. Sit down and write out the requirements of that job as far as you know them. A job ad, which is really a mini-job description, is the ideal place to start.

By way of example, here's a phrase from a recent job advertisement: "Persistence, enthusiasm, leadership, and team-building skills will enable the right individual to realize the full potential of this opportunity."

A lot of people applying for this job will tell the interviewer that they're persistent, and enthusiastic, and able to put together effective teams.

Far more memorable, though, will be those job applicants who come up with a story about their past work experience (or even volunteer or extra-curricular experience) that graphically illustrates how their persistence paid off, or how teams they put together met deadlines, or how their leadership abilities helped complete a tough project.

> You have to use the "I" word.

Key to the success of this approach is that each story relate a specific incident. Too often, there's a tendency to speak in generalities, such as: "As a manager, I've always been able to pull effective teams together."

While that statement has slightly more impact than the statement "I'm a team builder," it pales beside a story of an actual incident.

Here's an example:

"I was asked to head up a task force to examine how our company could get on the environmental band wagon and eliminate some of the paper and printing waste that plagued the organization.

"Another manager had already come to me with some suggestions, so I wanted her on the team. I went to the administration manger and asked him to recommend two more people. I told him I wanted people who were naturally efficient.

"We met three or four times to decide on things like areas of inquiry, and process. Then I assigned each member, myself included, to investigate one of them and come up with recommendations.

"Our report was accepted in total by senior management and virtually all our recommendations accepted. In the first year, the company cut its paper needs by 20 per cent and its printing bill by about 15 per cent."

If you often leave job interviews annoyed with yourself, feeling that you haven't given the person interviewing you a clear sense of your abilities, devote some time to developing situation/action/benefit stories.

Though it takes some planning, once mastered, this story-telling approach can help you leave interviews knowing you've presented yourself accurately and fully.

Bosses may not be trained
to ask the right questions

"I do okay when interviewers know what they're doing and ask the right questions," a job seeker said recently. "But I'm lost when they don't.

"My last interview was a real letdown," she continued. "I spent a lot of time preparing, for nothing. I think the guy liked me. He told me a lot about the job. But he never really asked me what I could do. I didn't get a chance to tell him."

These days, it can take months of effort to get one interview. Having that interview fall flat because of lack of skill on the part of the interviewer can be extremely discouraging.

"Just how much control do I have in an interview?" this job seeker asked. "I wanted to take over, but I didn't dare."

Though a lot has been written on the subject, there's no consensus on interview etiquette — what works, what doesn't; what's acceptable, what isn't.

Subject, as they are, to so many variables, interviews are hard to predict. This makes them somewhat difficult to prepare for, too, though not impossible. And, as this reader discovered, simply being prepared to answer questions is not always enough.

People trained in interview techniques know how to probe and keep probing until they get a clear sense of your abilities. But you can't count on always being interviewed by an expert.

"Employers ... may be much better at running their firms than they are at interviewing," Robert Wegmann and Robert Chapman write in their book *The Right Place At The Right Time.* "Some interview only rarely. Most have no formal training at it. What they really want is to hire someone good ... and then get back to running the business."

Taking over an unfocused and rambling interview to offer specific information about your abilities can work to your advantage, Wegmann and Chapman say. But be sure to do it subtly. "Focus on the employer's needs and your ability to meet them," they advise. "Be prepared to raise any essential topics that the employer might miss. If the employer leaves the interview with detailed information about you and your ability to do the job, and he does not have this information about other candidates, you are more likely to be offered the position."

In their book, Wegmann and Chapman suggest that as you prepare for interviews, you think of them as having five stages. You can manage each stage, they say.

• At the outset, there's introductory chatting to establish rapport. This stage is more important than people often realize, the authors contend. They advise that you be open and friendly; that you maintain eye contact; that you look for common ground.

• As the interview moves into the second stage, which the authors call "discussing the demands of the position," they suggest you remain actively involved. You're not the focus of the discussion at this stage, the job

> "Employers may be much better at running their firms than they are at interviewing."

is. "Even if you have a good idea of what the position requires, you want to hear the person who will supervise your work spell out, in her own words, what she wants you to do," they write.

• Once you're clear about the employer's needs, move into stage three — summarizing what the interviewer said. Use a phrase like: "If I understand you correctly, what you're looking for is someone who can...." Summarizing in this way is key, the authors say. It not only shows that you listen well, it enables you to clear up any misunderstandings. It also tells the employer that you take what's been said seriously. And it allows you to further assess whether this is the right job for you.

• If you feel it is, you can move easily into the fourth stage of the interview, describing your skills, personality and experience. "Your goal is to tell the employer everything about yourself that fits what you have just heard," Wegmann and Chapman write. "Omitting anything irrelevant, review your job-related natural aptitudes (with examples). Summarize your prior work experience, emphasizing the quality of your work and what you learned from it.... Make it clear, point by point, that you have the ability and experience to do this job unusually well."

The fifth stage of the actual interview, according to Wegmann and Chapman, is expressing enthusiasm and closing.

That's not the end of it, they add. Interviews, especially those that you've handled in this proactive way because you feel you're the right person for the job, should be followed with a letter. It's not only polite, the authors say, it also gives you a chance to re-state some of the positive points you made during the interview and cover additional points you failed to mention.

There's no magical, foolproof way to make sure that an interview will go the way you planned. This method, which Chapman and Wegmann take care to point out takes a lot of practice and planning, won't work in highly structured interviews, for example.

But in interviews with managers and supervisors who have had little interview training, it can help give you a sense of control over the information exchange.

Preparing for a panel interview

The question hangs in the air like an expectant cloud, filling every corner of the room. You pause, gathering your thoughts. Three pair of eyes watch. Three pens, poised over official-looking forms, wait to interpret your answer, record your score.

Most people find traditional one-on-one interviews stressful enough. Panel interviews, or *selection boards*, as they're often called, turn the heat up a notch further.

Presenting yourself fully while fielding questions from several people is no easy task.

Yet, if you're building a career in government, in a Crown corporation or in a large institution — a hospital or college, for example — there's generally no escaping selection board interviews. At some point, especially as you move up the ladder, you're going to have to meet, and impress, a panel of people whose job it is to assess you, your background and abilities against prescribed criteria.

Generally, two, three or four people sit on a board — the manager, a technical expert (if the manager isn't one), perhaps someone from a related department, or a human resources representative. Increasingly, care is taken to assure boards have male and female representation and employment equity representation.

Once a selection board has been established, members meet to discuss the needs of the position, the climate of the organization and what is required to "fit" with the team, says Claudette Belize, a staffing consultant for the federal government.

Once "screening criteria" have been set, Belize says, your application must meet them — things like education, experience, security (clearance) levels, language requirements and occupational certification — or you won't get an interview.

The board will also decide upon "assessment criteria and weighting," Belize says. "How much importance they're going to give to this factor as opposed to that factor."

Another human resource specialist described the rating process this way: "Factors are set up in relation to their importance in performing the job. If it's a position in a data centre, computer skills would be the number one factor. For a research position, attention to detail might be the number one factor. If you also have to work as part of a team, interpersonal skills would be the next factor."

> A fair way to ensure objectivity, or a bureaucratic way to spread the decision-making process?

If you've ever been interviewed by a selection board, you'll know that one of the most nerve-wracking aspects is that throughout, people are assessing what you say. They're either scribbling furiously or thoughtfully noting the scores they've assigned to your responses.

At the close of the interview, board members get together and, collectively, rate you on each factor and tally your results.

Getting the highest score doesn't necessarily win you the job, either. Other factors sometimes come into play — the seniority of other applicants, for instance.

Some job seekers maintain that intimidation is the motive behind selection board interviews. "I call it the inquisition style," wrote Karen in a letter to *Career Monitor*. "I've been interviewed by as few as four people and as many as 12."

While it is possible that some people get a power boost from sitting on a selection board and firing questions at nervous job seekers, as often as not this type of interview amounts to little more than a bureaucratic way to spread the decision-making process among several people.

Those who use the procedure defend it. Interviews of this kind "ensure consistency and objectivity," says Claudette Belize. Consensus must be reached, so "they're fairer. They provide a more accurate portrait of the individual," she says.

Preparation, information and practice can help relieve the stress of panel interviews. Here are some tips and suggestions:

Find out as much as you can about the position.
Internal candidates will find this easier than external ones. Get hold of a job description or job advertisement. Get the department manager's name and call for more information.

Prepare fully.
The more you do, the less stress you'll feel. Know all the qualifications required in the job. Be ready to discuss, in detail, your background and how it relates to each qualification.

Listen carefully to the instructions.
Selection board interviews are highly structured. The format of the interview will be outlined at the outset.

Give detailed responses to each question.
If you know one or two people on the board, don't assume their knowledge of you and your work will carry to other members of the group.

Direct your answers to the person who asked the question.
Look at and respond to each of the questioners in turn. Glance occasionally at other board members to include them. If you feel a rapport with one member of the panel, be careful not to deal with just that person.

If a question isn't posed clearly, ask for clarification.
Not all interviewers are equal. Some are bright and outgoing and word their questions well. Others are not as well prepared, or as articulate.

Be a good listener.
Don't let nervousness or apprehension cause you not to listen carefully to each question. There's nothing wrong with taking 30 seconds or so to reflect or to organize your thoughts.

Be prepared for "behavior-based" questions.
These are questions worded like: "What would you do in this situation?" or "What did you do in a similar situation?" They're designed to draw you out.

Practise.
Get a friend to ask you, again and again, to explain how your background and abilities are relevant to each requirement for the job.

Interviews with executive recruiters

Take a walk on the streets of almost any major city during the working day and you're bound to see them. Well groomed, briefcases in hand, their scars are hidden.

Perhaps they're heading to the office they use at an outplacement firm, or maybe to a job interview. They might be going to meet an executive recruiter or "search consultant," as they prefer to be called at the upper end of the recruiting spectrum.

They are out-of-work executives.

They look much the same as they did when walking the plush carpets of the executive floor. But they're devastated at finding themselves on the job market after years with one company, and often quite unaware of how to look for work in the '90s.

> "The relationship is a business relationship. It's give and take, not 'Here I am, help me out.'

A senior executive bumped from a job can have as much trouble as anybody else finding work; in some cases, more. Used to exercising power and giving direction, some executives find it difficult to go to others and ask for help, or advice, or a job.

A case in point: Senior people often don't know how to work effectively with executive search consultants, says Michael Wolkensperg, a partner and director of executive search with the Phillips Group of Companies.

Wolkensperg, who sometimes gives seminars on the topic to unemployed executives, says only about 20 per cent of one's job-search activities should be focused on executive recruiters and search consultants. And there are ways, he says, to manage and get the most from those relationships.

Too often, executives approach the consultant with unrealistic expectations, Wolkensperg says. "They'll come in and say, `Here I am. This is me. This is what I've done. This is what I want. Now what?'

"And that's not our role at all," he says.

"The relationship between a candidate and a search consultant is a business relationship, it's give and take, rather than 'Here I am, help me out.' Don't expect a consultant to take over your life, package you."

Search consultants and executive recruiters don't provide placement service to executives. The executive is not the client (as he or she is probably used to being). The hiring organization is the client. The consultant is that organization's recruiting agent. The way to get to the organization is to persuade the consultant of your suitability.

The best approach, in Wolkensperg's view, is "promoting rather than selling. People who say `Here I am and this is what I can do,' are selling," he says. "They are responding to their own needs. Promoting is more `Let's talk together. What's the problem that needs to be solved? How can I solve it?' (When somebody approaches me that way) they're responding to my needs."

Wolkensperg looks for people who can talk easily about themselves, their circumstances and their abilities. He respects, as well, those who are "comfortable with their shortcomings. People shouldn't try to pretend that they don't have any," he says. "I call it knowing oneself. If it's a real shortcoming, I want to know what they're doing about it; if it's a weakness they're going to have for the rest of their life, how they've learned not to depend on it."

No matter how comfortable you feel with a consultant, keep in mind at all times that this is a "business exchange." Don't go in looking for comfort. "My job is not to make you feel better," Wolkensperg says. "My job is to put you at ease, so that I can get to know you."

There is never, in Wolkensperg's view, a perfect job candidate. When presenting a short list to his client, he doesn't rate the candidates Rather, he says, "this is where this person is going to win for you, and this is where you need to watch out. Each candidate is presented as having a basket of solutions and a basket of problems.

"The question the employer has to answer is, 'Which basket am I most comfortable with?'"

Although he deals exclusively with senior executives, on several points Wolkensperg's advice is relevant to job hunters at all levels.

Say you've been fired. When asked in an interview why you're unemployed, Wolkensperg advises, don't offer the gritty details. "It's interesting, but it has zip to do with what we're discussing.

"I want to know how you handled the fallout. I want to hear: `I got out-gunned. It wasn't pleasant, but I learned from it. This is what I can do...."

And never discuss your age, Wolkensperg adds, offering encouraging news to those worrying about being "too old." Age is a "non-issue," he maintains. "Don't even bring it up. You only harm yourself. An old person is someone who is always responding instead of looking at the world with wonder. You're only old if you feel old, if you think of yourself as old.

"I'm getting requests today for people with `battle scars,'" he adds. Some employers are saying, 'I want somebody who's made those mistakes. I don't want them to learn on my time.'"

To find a search consultant, particularly one who is a specialist in your industry, talk to senior people in your field and get recommendations, Wolkensperg advises. Executives who put some effort into building a business relationship with a consultant, he adds, will discover a valuable career management resource.

Chapter 10

COPING
WITH
STRESS

BRIAN HUGHES

Turn your anxiety into action

Looking for work is never exactly fun. In times like these, it's even more draining than usual. Still, the stress of unemployment is "situational." Once you're working again, it will disappear. As long as you're still knocking on doors, though, it requires some management.

"Stress is the feeling our bodies experience when reacting biochemically to new demands," say Frederick DeRoche and Mary McDougall in their guide for "outplaced" employees called *Now It's Your Move* (Prentice Hall, Inc.).

People respond to these new demands in different ways, the authors believe. Stress can be either energizing or debilitating, they suggest, depending on how it affects the behavior of the person experiencing it.

> "Planning can minimize the amount of stress that you experience."

Their point is well taken. Even in adverse times, some people are activated by job loss. It provides the push they needed to do something different and change their lives. People like this hit the ground running and conduct an active job search until they're re-employed.

Others, those who were really attached to their jobs, for example, or those who were totally surprised at being fired, often find the demands of unemployment overwhelming. Once the shock wears off, bitterness and recrimination take over. Or they slip so deeply into depression and apathy that they can't seem to get going.

Still others panic, and begin running about applying for every job that comes up, whether they're qualified or not, setting themselves up for rejection — and more stress.

In fairness, finding yourself unemployed when jobs are at a premium is bound to be distressing. But attitude is vitally important.

So is preparation. In fact, planning for the period you're unemployed is key to managing stress, DeRoche and McDougall write. It "doesn't make this time free of stress ... but it can minimize the amount of stress that you experience."

As a first step, deal with the realities of your financial circumstances. Sit down with pen and paper and assess the money coming in against that going out. Even those who receive severance pay often find belt tightening necessary. Talk to your creditors. It may be possible to work out lower payments until you're working again.

Use this time to assess your career path to date. Are you on the right track? Does your work interest you? Does it use your best skills? Do you have other skills you'd like to use as well?

Whether you choose a new field or decide to pursue the one you're in, research it thoroughly. Is it growing or shrinking? What are the opportunities? (Yes, there are opportunities, even in a tough economy.) Would additional training help you take advantage of them? What does the future hold?

As best you can, develop a concrete career plan. Once in place, it will alleviate some of the uncertainty. At the same time, a highly targeted job search gives you a sense of control. It also impresses employers.

Some experts suggest that you make your job search your full-time job. You may find this excessive and decide to set aside a portion of each week to do the personal things you never had time for when you were working every day. It is true, though, that by creating a daily routine and following it, you can re-create, to a certain extent, the structure that disappeared along with your job.

Set up a work area from which to make calls. Keep job search records organized. Develop a follow-up system that works. At the beginning of each week, set an agenda. Do your best to stick to it. Again, it will give you a sense of control.

The people close to you can help you manage stress, as well. Just being able to tell someone how you feel, being able to get things off your chest, can be helpful. Those people in your support system who are dependent on you may be feeling as insecure as you are. Open the lines of communication and keep them open.

Don't be afraid to ask for suggestions and help.

Maintain regular exercise. Walking, jogging, sports of all kinds can help relieve tension. Meditation and other relaxation techniques are also helpful. If you'd like more information on these, there are lots of books and tapes on the subject in libraries and book stores.

Above all, keep in mind that the trough you're in is temporary. There is a job out there for you. With concerted effort, you'll find it, and finding your next job is the very best way to ease the stress of unemployment.

Nobody said it would be easy

Looking for work is only part looking. The other part is waiting. Waiting for the phone to ring. Waiting for decisions to be made. Waiting for life to regain the order that comes from having a job to go to every day.

Some job seekers are experiencing insensitive, inconsiderate, even rude treatment these days. It doesn't happen all the time, they say, but often enough to erode what — for some — is already shaky confidence.

Many employers and recruiters are self-absorbed in times like these. "They aren't very sensitive to the plight of the unemployed," observed one out-of-work executive. "They're hounded. They're getting so many resumes, so many calls."

This lack of sensitivity makes job hunting even more difficult than usual. One needs a thick skin, tenacity, and an unwavering positive attitude.

One of the most frustrating aspects of her own job search has been the "hurry-up-and-wait syndrome," says Janet R., a marketing manager with 10 years' experience who is trying to change career direction.

"You get a call about a job, and it's urgent," she explains. "Everything has to happen within 48 hours. So you rush to meet all their deadlines. And then you wait. Weeks can go by before you hear anything."

> "It's urgent. So you rush to meet all their deadlines. And then you wait. Weeks can go by before you hear anything."

Paul M., with nearly 20 years' experience in property management, concurs. He tells of the employer who called his home one day when he was out. "He left word that he had to meet me right away," Paul recalls. "He left phone numbers for his office, his home and his car so I could reach him.

"When I did reach him, he said things were moving very quickly, could I come down? So I rushed down," Paul says. "He said he'd get back to me by the end of the week. He didn't. I called. He said he'd get back to me by the middle of the next week. He didn't. I called again. He said, 'It's down to you and a property management company.'

"I was astounded. All this hurry-up business and he was still considering contracting the work out! He should have made that decision before he started interviewing people."

Inconsiderate? Yes. Rude? Yes.

And stories like this abound these days. When there are more people looking for work than there are jobs, it's a buyer's market. As a job seeker, you're generally unknown to the people you approach. You're easy to forget, easy to ignore.

"It gets really disheartening," Janet R. says. "It's the frustration. You know you've got the skills, you've got the talent, you've got the drive, you've got the know-how. You could really help build a good business and get things going. And people just aren't responding. It's hard."

Janet has categorized the employers she's met over the past year into three groups.

• First, there are the phenomenally busy people who are genuinely considerate but who have time commitments that make it impossible for them to get back to their calls. "When they do phone, they are very apologetic, very understanding," she says. "After the first or second time, they turn it around and say, 'Keep calling me.'"

• Secondly, there are the people, busy as well, who want to appear considerate, but who really aren't. "They've gotten caught up in their world and they've forgotten what it's like to be on the other side, to be waiting for that call," Janet believes. When you do finally reach them, after papering their wall with messages, "they're short or abrupt," she adds.

• The third type, says Janet, are "arrogant bastards. I hate to say that because it's a negative term," she says, "but I don't know what else to call them. They think so highly of themselves and that they have so much power. They care nothing for the people they're interviewing. They treat them like garbage."

Employers aren't the only ones guilty of inconsiderate behavior. Paul M. tells of the shabby treatment he received from "a reputable, well-known head hunter."

> "When I was on their short list they couldn't do enough for me. When I wasn't the leading candidate, it was like I had the plague."

"I had a panel interview. I guess it didn't go my way," Paul says. "But they (the recruiting firm) never got back to me. Not a phone call, or a letter. I'd had two or three meetings with them, made two or three trips downtown. And they didn't even have the courtesy to send me a letter, thank me for my attendance and let me know the position had been filled.

"It reminded me of the song *Smiling Faces*," he continues. "When I was on their short list, they couldn't do enough for me, they couldn't send me enough information. Everything was sent out by courier. When I wasn't the leading candidate, it was like I had the plague or AIDS. They wouldn't even return my calls."

There's no question that recruiters are beleaguered in times like these. Still, such realities shouldn't preclude common courtesy and basic business etiquette. So says Pierre W., who until last year was vice-president and chief operating officer for a division of a large conglomerate.

"It's a question of basic good manners, of consideration for another human being," he says.

Some might disagree, and insist that business priorities outweigh such minor concerns. Pierre sticks to his guns, recalling his recent opportunity to experience recruitment American-style. It's far preferable, he says.

"I responded to a box number for a general manager and got a call from a recruiting firm in Chicago," Pierre recalls. "A very pleasant man made an appointment with me for the following week. He was on time. He was very direct and open. He went right through the resume in an absolutely thorough way.

"He told me exactly when he would call. And he did. He told me it had been down to three people and that I had been one of them. He advised that the company had picked an individual and they would be making an offer next week. He told me a bit about the man's background and why they were making this decision. He said he'd get back to me if it didn't go through.

"It was totally professional," he adds. "I didn't feel like I'd been used in any sense. I felt I'd had an opportunity to present what I had to offer."

Though anecdotal evidence only, stories like these paint a grim picture of the Canadian scene. But is it the whole picture?

"I don't think anyone is crassly dealing with people or wilfully being unfair or bad-mannered," says Doug Caldwell of Caldwell Partners. But business is down, it's harder to conduct, and the volume of people looking for work is, at times, overwhelming, he says.

Calls to several recruiters found that the economy has them in a tight squeeze. There aren't that many jobs around.

Despite the numbers of unemployed, business is slow and costs have to be kept down accordingly. In some recruiting firms this has meant layoffs. At the very least, it has meant that additional staff can't be hired.

And additional staff is what's needed to handle the number of people knocking on recruiters' doors these days. A couple of years ago a recruiting ad would typically draw 100 or, at the most, 200 replies. Today, there can be upwards of 500.

Many of those applying are unemployed and have been for months, so they're more aggressive and demanding, recruiters say. "Now they mail a resume, they call us, and fax us," one recruiter explained. "Our systems aren't up to it. Some people fall through the cracks."

Employers, not job seekers, are a recruiter's clients. And those clients are extremely specific and very picky in a buyer's market. They want to "shop," and to keep shopping until they find the absolutely perfect candidate. It's not uncommon for the specifications on any particular job to change halfway through a search, recruiters say.

When that happens, further screening is required. The recruiting process slows down even more. Decisions are pushed back; backlogs occur.

And phone calls aren't returned.

Be that as it may, it doesn't change anything for people like Janet R. and Paul M., waiting for good news, bad news, any news. They have little left to do but grow more frustrated, more demoralized, and more indignant.

"I'm not a moaner or complainer," says Janet. "I just want to be dealt with professionally. Just do what you say you'll do," she pleads. "And, be fair."

It's shortsighted not to be, Paul adds. "I'm a senior manager and a potential source of business. There's a couple of recruiters in this city who will never get business from me."

Janet and Paul, both now working after nearly a year of looking, agree that it's almost impossible not to take such treatment personally. It not only affects them and their self-esteem, it affects the people around them.

"You're so emotionally involved in a job search," Paul explains. "You try not to let it bother you but it's hard to distance yourself from it. It impacts on your whole family."

> "You're so emotionally involved. You try not to let it bother you but it's hard to distance yourself."

As his job search wore on, Paul became more outspoken. When another prospective employer began the pattern of not calling when he said he would, Paul confronted him. "I called him and said, `You said you'd call and you didn't. I'm losing faith. Are you serious or not?'

"You get overly sensitive," he admits ruefully.

"That was a low point and a high point," Paul adds. "Because I got the position."

When looking for work, you're vulnerable and exposed. Too often, you're at the whim of busy and/or insensitive people who have never been unemployed or who have forgotten what it's like.

When you encounter such people, your options are limited. You can simply put up with it, and decide not to take it personally. You can confront them, as Paul did. You can decide to strike them off your list of potential employers, knowing that they aren't the kind of people you'd want to work with anyway.

And you can hope against hope that this kind of unprofessional, self-centred behavior will come back to haunt them.

Job loss puts a heavy strain on the family

Nothing can throw lives into a tailspin like the loss of a job.

As the unemployed person spins around and around, looking for a place to land, everyone else involved — kids, parents, mate, even friends — spins around too.

To date, little recognition has been given to the devastating effect job loss has on a family. For the individual, getting fired is a career crisis. If it isn't handled well, however, it can easily precipitate a family crisis.

> "We want women
> to know
> that their
> feelings are
> normal."

Two Toronto consultants, Jill Jukes and Ruthan Rosenberg, have written a book on the subject called *I Got Fired Too: Coping With Your Husband's Job Loss* (Stoddart Press).

Although the authors have a lot to say about the pressure job loss puts on all kinds of relationships, in the book they talk specifically to wives — which makes sense. Major wage earners today are still mostly male. And when a husband loses a job, no one spins faster, in the same whirlwind with him, than his wife.

Generally, it's the wife who works behind the scenes to keep her family on track when a disaster like this strikes. She learns to cope as she goes. Rosenberg and Jukes are among the first professionals to talk directly to these women. Their book strives to tell them, in some detail, what to expect and how to manage.

"We want women to know that their feelings are normal," says Jukes. "We want them to know that what they're experiencing is understandable. It's predictable. It's manageable. It's survivable."

I Got Fired Too is based on interviews with 52 women married to men who'd been fired. As they describe their experiences in poignant detail, their stories open a window on to the complicated, often conflicting, emotions that characterize personal relationships during a crisis.

"I was mad at him," one woman is quoted as saying. "You want to blame somebody, and in the back of your mind you're thinking, What the heck did he do? Why did he let this happen? So there is anger toward your husband, then guilt that you are mad at him.... You have to keep it inside, because this is not the time to get mad. He's so devastated and so fragile that if you come out and attack him you won't solve anything."

The book is written from the perspective of people at the upper end of the earning spectrum. Still, most anyone who has lived through a major job loss will relate to what these 52 women have to say. In many ways, *I Got Fired Too* is a how-to manual for families, charting the sometimes lengthy transition from one job to another.

Both Jukes and Rosenberg work in the outplacement business. In one highly informative chapter, they de-mystify the job search process, showing the wife — whom they describe as an "invisible partner" in the job search — how she can help.

Everyone reacts differently to crisis situations. Everyone finds different ways to cope. Managing something like this successfully will depend on all sorts of things — an ability to plan, the strength of the relationship, previous experience with crisis. But mostly, the authors say, it will depend on a couple's ability to communicate with each other.

Jukes tells of one woman who put it this way: "One of the reasons we are being successful is that we talked and talked and talked. I listened until I was sick of listening. But I listened."

> "There is anger toward your husband, then guilt that you are mad at him. You have to keep it inside."

"Whenever there was a marriage breakdown," Rosenberg adds, "it was a breakdown in communication."

Couples experiencing a job loss are wise to "open lines of communication early," Rosenberg suggests. "Begin talking about the practical issues of job search. The spouse needs to know what her husband's job target is. What his goals are. What his criteria are."

It will also be helpful to raise the question of "How do we talk about this to our children?" Rosenberg continues. "What do we say? How can we help them? How do we talk to family? How do we talk to friends?"

Above all, she concludes, people need to ask: "How can we do this together? What can we do to help each other?"

Job loss throws a couple into a "parallel crisis," Jukes explains. "He's going down one track and she's going down another. It's not easy to get across to his track and to get into his head. A wife will literally have to make a conscious effort to put whatever she's dealing with aside. Her husband has to do that for her. At times, they'll have to tell each other that that's what they need."

Working together to find new employment can strengthen a relationship. At the same time, it can give a woman a sense of personal confidence. Says Rosenberg: "Nothing will make a woman feel better than having come through something like this to say: 'I learned, I grew, I managed. It was tough, but I did it.'"

TIP

"Financial worries can erode the effectiveness of a job search," says career consultant John Hamilton. "If you lose a job, don't leave your finances in a worrisome state. Consciously trim your sails. Have a succession of financial fall-back plans to deal with worst-case scenarios, thus arranging for a long 'financial leash.'"

Chapter 11

SUPPORT SYSTEMS

BRIAN HUGHES

Group helps workers search for jobs

I t's a large room, and virtually all the seats are taken. The meeting's about to start. There's a buzz of conversation and a palpable energy in the room. Notes are being compared, names exchanged. This is a weekly meeting of the Executive Advancement Resource Network. EARN, as it's called, is a Toronto self-help group of unemployed managers, professionals and executives. Faced with the limited impact of political and bureaucratic policies on the daunting employment scene, some displaced workers are turning to groups like these to develop their own resources and explore alternatives.

EARN exists because Colleen Clarke lost her job. Just nine months earlier, she says, she'd changed careers, moving from sales and marketing promotional events into leasing retail space in malls and shopping centres.

> "There's got to be other people out there. We could get together, share information and be a support system for one another."

Like many people, after five months of job hunting and several rejections, Clarke felt stuck. "My networking sources had dried up," she recalls. "I didn't know what to do anymore. I didn't know where to look.

"I thought, there's got to be other people out there. We could get together, share information and be a support system for one another. It came to me that I should form a group, a little group that would meet in my living room."

That was then. Now, EARN has about 350 members. And Clarke's living room has been replaced by this meeting room at an uptown library.

Timing is one thing that contributed to EARN's success. Another is Clarke's considerable energy and her emphasis on the importance of a positive attitude. "You can't get anywhere in life with a bad attitude," she says with conviction.

Clarke opens the meeting with a question. "Did anyone get a job this week?" At the back of the room, a hand goes up. A clean-cut, well-dressed fellow comes to the front to address the group.

"At first, I didn't know what to think about broadcast letters," he admits. "But nothing else was working much, so I tried one.

"And it worked. I got a call for a meeting. It went very well. Then I got a call for another meeting. And last week, a final interview. I start work in three weeks."

He sits down to a round of sincere applause.

"One broadcast letter. One," quips Clarke to an appreciative crowd, many of whom have sent hundreds of such marketing letters.

It's not unusual for communities to pull together during times of adversity. Bringing together a community of unemployed people in a large urban centre can be difficult, however. In Clarke's case, media interest and support made it possible, she says.

Similar groups have subsequently sprung up in a number of other centres, both urban and suburban.

Such self-help groups of unemployed workers are a product of our time, says Jim Ratcliffe, organizer of Network 91 — Managers in Transition. "As the economy picks up," he believes, "they'll phase out."

"It's really networking," says Colleen Clarke. "You have a room of a hundred people who've worked for however many companies and know however many people. Everyone keeps their eyes and ears open for everyone else."

Self esteem improves with HUGS

By the time Steve S. found his way into a Handling Unemployment Group, he was nearing his breaking point.

"I was really in trouble," Steve recalls. "Everything was happening all at once. I was losing my unemployment (insurance). I was going to lose my car — I've always had a car, all my life. I was starting to think: 'I guess I'm a lazy, good-for-nothing.'

"You start losing a sense of the value of your experience, you start questioning, `What good is it?'" explains Steve, a self-described "jack of all trades" whose versatility is both a blessing and a curse, he says.

Over a period of 14 months, Steve had applied for hundreds of jobs, from "sales and plant management on the high end, to pumping gas on the low end." Nothing had come his way, however, and months of unsuccessful job hunting have taken their toll.

"You start feeling worthless," he says.

Helping people cope with such feelings is what Handling Unemployment Groups (HUG) is all about. It's a community-based program in which people get together nine times over a three or four-week period. They meet in small groups — never more than 15, to discuss problems, look for solutions, and to help each other come to grips with being unemployed during these trying times.

Dedicated to the concept of mutual support, HUG's underlying premise is that the people best able to understand what you go through when you're unemployed are those who find themselves in the same spot.

HUG is not about getting people jobs, says program consultant and trainer Roni Chaleff. Rather, it's about helping people learn how to deal with the stress that comes when you lose a job and can't find another one.

"People take an emotional beating when they're unemployed," explains Chaleff. "How long can you go on? How can your ego handle another rejection? You get to the point where you want to give up.

"So when they come to these groups, it's a breath of fresh air for them.

"We allow people the chance to explore their feelings, and to come up with coping strategies. No one says, 'Come on, pull up your bootstraps, get out there, try it one more time.' We say, 'Here you can talk about what it really feels like.'"

> "No one says,'Come on, pull up your bootstraps, get out there, try it one more time.' We say, 'Here you can talk about what it really feels like.'"

HUG provided Steve with the outlet he needed. "It got me to talk more, to get it off my chest instead of letting it eat me up," he says. "I let off a lot of steam there."

There are other important side benefits, according to Chaleff.

People are able to share experiences and feel less isolated, they learn to understand the economic conditions that caused their unemployment and, ultimately, they find it easier to muster the considerable energy job hunting takes.

In HUG sessions, discussion focuses on topics such as stress, decision making, goal setting, relaxation, coping techniques and time management. More traditional job search concerns — interviews, networking, resume writing — are discussed as well, Chaleff adds, but HUG counsellors come at those issues in a slightly different way.

"We don't say, `This is how you do it, go do it,'" Chaleff explains. "We say, 'If you're afraid of interviewing, or of networking, let's look at why you're afraid. How can we break down some of the stereotypes? How can we make it more positive for you?'"

Steve appreciated that approach. "They don't put anything into you," he explains. "They want you to say it. They want you to see your strong points."

Through this process, Steve came to understand that he's at his best, and happiest, when training others, helping them learn new skills. He's looking for a job that will allow him to do that.

HUG was first developed as a response to the high levels of unemployment caused in the recession in 1981-82. As the employment scene improved during the last half of the '80s, the need for support groups like this lessened, and the HUG program was phased out.

When the economy slumped again in the early '90s, the Ontario Ministry of Health, with nearly $1 million from a provincial government anti-recession grant, dusted HUG off, contracted with community employment services and began sponsoring these support groups in some 18 centres in southern Ontario.

HUG is for people who are unemployed, actively looking for work, and in need of some emotional support. It can't provide career counselling, training or job placement, although HUG counsellors may be able to refer people to other community services.

I am a 25-year-old unemployed male. I have been unemployed for more that a year and a half. I am at a point where my self-esteem is very low. Sometimes I am very frustrated. Being unemployed for a long time has many drawbacks. I am losing confidence in myself.

I have received rejection after rejection. I have lost all hope of finding a job. Maybe some people are just born winners or born losers. Unfortunately, I belong to the latter classification

Janis Foord Kirk
Career Monitor

AND IN REPLY

Please, please try not to take the rejection you're experiencing personally. So many other qualified people are experiencing it too. It's especially difficult, I know, for young people with few career successes to their credit.

Try to connect with a support group in your community. To find one, check with your regional community services department. You might check, as well, with a community college, or with your local Canada Employment Centre.

Chapter 12

CHANGING
STRIDES

Raffi Anderian *

*Graphic reprinted with permission — The Toronto Star Syndicate

Losing a job can mean winning yourself

I t was with mixed emotions that Vicki V., a marketing professional, learned that she'd lost her job. Not only did it come out of the blue, it was handled callously. "It was horrible," she recalls, then adds ironically, "and the best thing that ever happened to me."

Once the shock wore off, Vicki was able to acknowledge that her work situation and her boss had demoralized her, and that she was well rid of both. With determination and a relentlessly positive attitude, she set about rebuilding her life.

Today, at 39, Vicki is on a very different path. Her previous career was played out in the arena of two highly traditional, corporate settings — retail and publishing. Since being fired, she's come to realize that the corporate world no longer appeals to her. Nor, she suspects, does it have a place for her.

> "Everything is step-by-step building. If you keep at it, it can be done."

Venturing into uncharted, entrepreneurial territory — especially during one of the toughest economic periods in decades — took a lot of courage. "It's hard," she admits. "But everything is step-by-step building. If you keep at it, it can be done."

Like many people, Vicki, an expert when it comes to marketing a product or service, had no idea how to market herself. From the time she started working, "I just kept moving on and moving up," she says. "I never had to do a resume in my life."

Still, her marketing instincts are strong. Without really seeing it as a marketing venture, she began the process of evaluating her product — in this case, herself.

Inspiration and direction came (as it often has in her life, she says) from a book.

"I got *What Color Is Your Parachute?* (Ten Speed Press) and I went through it, page by page," Vicki recalls. "I did all the exercises. I filled out everything. I learned what I was good at, what I wasn't good at, what I liked doing, and that when I like doing something, I put a lot of enthusiasm into it."

She also learned that marketing was her forte and that, ultimately, she wanted her own business.

"It took me a long time to define my goals beyond that," she acknowledges. "But I did know I wanted to work with proactive, positive, successful people."

Vicki began seeking out such people and interviewing them for information. Career exploration to define a specific goal can be a lengthy process fraught with false starts and wrong turns. Vicki's quest was no different.

But she kept at it and eventually came up with a surprising goal for a woman with a retail and publishing background. Her specialty, Vicki decided, would be the small, competitive field of sports marketing.

"I do a lot of volunteer work and many of the projects and ideas I come up with are sports-minded," she explains. "In sports you set goals, you visualize. And it's a team environment. There's no star. I like that mentality."

Once she had her objective in mind, Vicki never lost sight of it. To make something happen for yourself, she believes, you have to prepare yourself mentally. It requires discipline.

She credits much of her success to the process of defining goals, writing them down, and visualizing them happening. That, and positive thinking.

"I've always believed in setting goals," she says. "Every book I've read says the same thing. You have to have goals, you have to write them down. That way you commit yourself to them.

"Every week, I clarify my goals. And I visualize them done."

Positive thinking has become a way of life for Vicki. She surrounds herself with positive people and stays away from those who aren't. "Every morning and every night, I do positive affirmations," she says, then quotes from the work of inspirational writer Napoleon Hill: "What the mind can conceive and believe, it can achieve."

The past year hasn't been without its struggles and setbacks, Vicki says. But whenever something held her back, she made an effort to face it head on and find a way around it.

Her fear of making "cold calls," for instance.

"I used to sit there, stare at the phone and say, `ring,'" she says with a chuckle. "Or I'd pick it up and start to dial, then I'd hang it up. It's so hard to call and break through secretaries. It's so hard not to take 'no' personally.

"I took on a couple of telephone sales and direct selling jobs specifically to get over that," she says. "It's one of the best lessons I've learned over the past few months."

Slowly, slowly, Vicki's efforts are paying off. She has her own marketing company now. Recently, she landed a contract, a big one, to promote a new sports venture —initially in Toronto, potentially across

Canada.

"It was an educational year," she says of the past year of personal evaluation, career exploration and struggling to make ends meet. "I've learned so much.

"I should be scared to death," she adds with a laugh. "But I feel great."

Paul Yachetti   PHOTO: KEVIN ARGUE

How one laid-off older worker
bounced back

Every Monday morning, long before the sun is up, Paul Yachetti leaves his comfortable, split-level home and drives six blocks or so to a sprawling, modern building near a busy highway.

At 4 a.m., surrounded by plants and the smell of damp earth, he starts work. This early morning shift is the first of three that Yachetti puts in each week in the warehouse at Westbrook Floral Ltd. He's there again on Wednesday and Thursday afternoons. Mostly, he works in the company's potted plant division, packaging plants for distribution to florists.

"I've always loved flowers and plants," he says. "But to identify them — it's an art in itself. I wasn't really good at it at first, but I'm getting better."

The fact is, Paul Yachetti has never worked at anything like this before.

Repairing moulds for making glass containers was Yachetti's job for more than 45 years. He's a skilled tradesman. He was shop foreman supervising 28 people in a large glass company's mould maintenance department when he retired.

Retiring wasn't his idea. At 62, Yachetti is vital and healthy. He loved his job. Like many senior workers today, he's the victim of circumstances beyond his control.

When Yachetti's employer merged with another company, a restructuring followed. Yachetti was among those who got the "golden nudge" — a severance package and an enhanced early retirement plan.

"Effective immediately," he says, shaking his head, as if still unable to believe it. "I felt I could have served a little longer. Especially with all the experience. But they don't look at it that way."

Nobody gets up and walks away from something like this unscathed. Yachetti handled it better than most, thanks in large part, he says, to the help he got from an outplacement consultant. "He told me it was like a death in the family. And he listened. I really needed someone that I could talk to."

> "I felt I could have served a little longer. But they don't look at it that way."

Despite that help, inactivity weighed heavily on Yachetti as the months passed. He missed the sense of identity work had given him. He missed being part of a community of workers.

"It's not really the money," he says. "It's doing something, belonging."

He decided to look for a part-time job. Such a simple decision, yet it threw Yachetti into uncharted territory.

Starting work in the 1940s was totally different than it is in the '90s. Yachetti's older brother had introduced him to the foreman at the glass company during the summer of 1942. He was just 13 at the time. That summer and the next, he worked nearly every day. He quit school in 1944 to work full-time.

Like so many others who spend their lives working for one employer, Yachetti had never looked for work before; never even been on a job interview.

Still, Paul Yachetti is one of those rare individuals who applies himself enthusiastically to everything he does. He found a job in just over a month after making, in total, about 18 job applications, he says.

With his positive attitude and engaging nature he succeeded, in spite of breaking most of the rules.

At his local library, Yachetti got books on resumes and "read a lot" but he "never made one out," he admits.

When answering ads, he seldom let the word "no" stop him. "A lot of times when I called they'd tell me, `I'm sorry, we have enough applications. We can't take any more,'" he says.

"I decided to ignore that and go down anyway. I'd say: `I have a lot of experience. I might be able to help your company.' And you know, they'd take my application. A couple of times, I got an interview that way."

Yachetti soon learned the importance of responding quickly. When he began looking for work, he'd wait until the first of the week to respond to an advertisement in the weekend paper. "On two or three occasions, by the time I got there, the job was already taken," he recalls.

Then, one Saturday morning, he saw an advertisement for part-time help at the floral warehouse.

"I thought, `I'll go down and see if they're open,'" he says. "The place was closed, but there was a car outside. So I walked in and found a gentleman sitting in the office. I told him I was looking for a job."

They talked for a while, Yachetti says, and he was told to come back Monday morning at 9. "I was there at 8:30," he chuckles.

P.J. Vermeer, the production manager, interviewed Yachetti just after 9 o'clock on that Monday morning. He hired him on the spot.

"It was Paul's attitude," says Vermeer. "It was as simple as that. He has a very positive, I-want-to-work attitude. It's very rare."

People like Paul Yachetti bring something important to today's rapidly changing workplace. Alternatives exist. It's easier to spot them if you're resourceful and positive and if you keep an open mind.

Career crisis brings new beginnings

"There are times when I say, `What have I gotten myself into?'" Andy Emmink admits. "But not that many. Mostly it's been a lot of fun."

The fun part, according to this self-employed businessman, was starting a business from scratch and making it work.

In 1988, more than 170,000 new businesses were started in Ontario alone — more than in any previous year. Accident Cost Management Services, Emmink's consulting firm, which helps employers manage their dealings with the Workers' Compensation Board, was one of them.

It's comforting to know, amid the steady stream of bankruptcies and foreclosures in recent years, that there are still firms out there, like Emmink's, doing very well indeed.

Running Accident Cost Management Services is Emmink's second career. He used to work for the Ontario Workers' Compensation Board, climbing the corporate ladder to become a director and secretary to the board.

It was a happy association, says Emmink, spanning nearly 20 years. During that time, few people, himself included, suspected that somewhere inside this self-described "career civil servant" lurked an entrepreneur.

It took a career crisis — the kind we're seeing more and more these days, to prompt Emmink to explore his potential. He was in a rut, he says. His job had "lost its challenge." Looking to the future, he saw only more of the same.

"I came to the realization that I'd given as much to the organization as I could and that the organization had given as much to me as it could," he says. "And I still had a good 20 years of working life left."

Emmink examined his alternatives and decided there were only three.

"I could continue in my job despite my conclusions," he said. "But I couldn't bear the thought of hitting retirement knowing I'd been sitting waiting to retire for 20 years."

His second option — to go to another employer — became his fallback.

Emmink chose option three. He decided to go into business for himself.

It wasn't an easy decision.

"Golden handcuffs" bound him to the Workers' Compensation Board, he says. And "there was a lot at stake. I had a wife, two children and a mortgage — like so many of us do. I was gambling with the livelihood of my family, and you don't take a thing like that lightly.

"Without my wife's support, I don't think I would have done it," he adds.

There's an air of competency and thoroughness about Andy Emmink. It's evident in the way he approached the task of setting himself up in business.

First, he assessed his market and found it viable. "There are about 200,000 employers in Ontario," Emmink says. "Even if 10 per cent of them are having some difficulties with the WCB, that's 20,000 potential clients."

Next, he bounced his consulting idea off four or five people outside the organization — not, he maintains, "just people who'd tell me what I wanted to hear."

Everyone he talked to encouraged him and Emmink increasingly began to apply himself to what he calls "the practicalities."

"I had to learn what's involved in setting up a business," he says. "I did a lot of research and reading. I talked to bankers and got them on side. Then I talked to accountants, and got that kind of expertise."

Despite the preparation, like most new entrepreneurs, Emmink learned his most valuable lessons on the job. "I didn't know that I actually had to go out and sell the service," he recalls with a chuckle. "I now realize I was naive. But after working at the WCB and knowing all the agony that was out there in the world of 'employerdom,' I thought I simply had to have a name in the phone book and they'd come beating down my door.

> "I thought I simply had to have a name in the phone book and they'd come beating down my door."

"I've had to become a salesman," he says. "It's taken up quite a bit of time, non-billable time. That was another surprise. When you first cost your potential income based on working a 40-hour week, you have dollar signs in your eyes. The reality is, you don't bill half of that — all your marketing and administration time is non-billable."

Two underlying traits are key to his entrepreneurial success, Emmink believes — stubbornness and self-discipline.

"On a beautiful summer day, you have the freedom to take the day off and go golfing or fishing. But you don't. You spend the time in your dark, dreary basement office looking through stacks of papers and calling prospective clients."

Those dreary days have paid off — so much so, in fact, that despite uncertain economic signals, Emmink expanded his operation. It was, in many ways, a leap of faith.

"At the time I made the decision the numbers said, don't do it," he admits. "But I've come to realize that if you wait until you can afford it, you never do it."

Emmink no longer runs Accident Cost Management Services from his basement office. The firm is now housed in a bright, modern space on the second floor of a low-rise suburban office building. He shares his new office with an assistant, Suzanne Cowan, whom he enticed away from the WCB. And this year, for the first time in three years, Emmink and his wife took a winter holiday.

Self-employment isn't the answer to everyone's career crisis.

As Emmink says, "it's a very personal decision." For him, though, it was the right decision. "I thoroughly enjoy what I'm doing. And there's been a 110 per cent reduction in stress level. There's a sense now that I have control over my own destiny."

TIP

"Accept that there is life beyond the corporate confines," suggests Andy Emmink. "There are a whole lot of opportunities out there that you've never considered. But you have to go and look for them. Get out and talk to people. Attend trade associations and luncheons. Meet people in private industry. You'll find there are a lot of people, probably with less cerebral capacity than you, making it and doing quite well for themselves."

If you decide to make the leap, though, "don't do it with blinkers on," Emmink cautions. "Understand that there are risks. Determine that you're going to succeed."

Successful consultants need marketing skills

By choice or circumstance, more and more people are moving into the consulting field these days. There's a receptive market for their services, says Kevin Hood, president of the fledgling Association of Independent Consultants (AIC).

"Consultant" is one of those words that can describe anything from an international merger-and-acquisition specialist to an out-of-work copywriter. In Hood's definition, however, a consultant is "self-employed and working for a wide range of clients."

It's a definite career choice, he says.

In these times of change, with the business world in such a state of uncertainty, a good many companies are struggling to find their way. "We are no longer playing by the same rules," Hood observes. "And, we're not sure what the rules are.

"The key is adaptability," he adds. "Companies have to be able to adjust. We're going to see a lot of sectoral recessions in the future as we adjust to the global economy. It's going to go on for a long time," Hood predicts.

"The global economy doesn't know what it needs yet."

To consultants like Hood, times of change like these mean business. "Take a domestic or North American-based company trying to change to a global marketing and sales structure," he says. "That company will have to go through incredible machinations in order to change people, attitudes, systems and structures. A consultant can help them short-cut the process ... and cut the development time in half."

As consultants move throughout the domestic and international marketplace, they see a wide array of companies struggling to survive and adapt, Hood says. "They see the lessons that have been learned, the mistakes that have been made and the positive moves companies have made to take advantage of opportunities that come along. They bring that knowledge to other companies."

> "The global economy doesn't know what it needs yet."

Consultants provide a valuable service to business owners and managers, allowing them to "pick a particular expertise without owning it," Hood suggests. "They can say, 'I need a trainer. I need a marketing expert. I need a financial expert. But I only need them for two weeks.'"

Hood, who bills himself as a "business and market development consultant," found his own career niche almost by accident. About five years ago, while looking for business opportunities, he came upon companies that needed his abilities, but only for a short time.

In his late 20s at the time, with a background in political administration and business development, Hood had no real understanding of how a consultant operates. As many consultants do, he learned the skills of his trade on his own, while on the job.

"I didn't know how to market myself, how not to give away my time, how to build a client base, and how to put together proposals," Hood recalls.

As the organizing force behind the Association of Independent Consultants, Hood's motives, initially, were self-serving. "I wanted to gain access to other people who were working independently and who had ideas, networks, and opportunities that I didn't have access to. I wanted to expand my horizons."

As he began talking to other independent consultants, however, Hood found that virtually everyone he spoke to had been wrestling with the same issues. As well, most had come to realize, along with Hood, that marketing was the key to their success.

"You always have to be developing business," Hood says. "Even when you're as busy as can be. It can never be off your mind."

Education to enhance consulting skills and adherence to professional standards have become key tenets of the AIC, says Hood. Members sign a code of ethics and commit to professional development.

Not everyone is prepared to put in the effort that's required, says Hood. "A lot of people out there fancy themselves as consultants. But when we present to them our organization and all the networking, training and marketing you have to do to become truly professional, they say, `I don't want to do that. I just want to get business. I came to your association because I want to get referrals.'"

> "You always have to be developing business."

These are not the kind of people needed in the consulting field, says Hood. "What the market needs is a wide range of very strong, well-educated, knowledgeable, and thorough consultants," he maintains.

Not to mention good marketers. If you have trouble selling yourself to others, beware. Because marketing is so important to success, consultants must "make a career of job hunting," Hood says.

BRIAN HUGHES

Do your homework
before working fromhome

Imagine: No more rush-hour traffic or over-crowded subway cars. No more boss looking over your shoulder. No more constant interruptions, or stale office air, or glaring fluorescent lights....

Who hasn't thought of working at home at least once? Increasingly, nowadays, a good many Canadians are doing more than just thinking about it. They're doing it, some on a part-time basis, others full-time.

If you're considering such a step, move cautiously. Test the waters carefully, says Douglas Gray.

A writer, lawyer and consultant, Gray is also something of an expert on work-at-home issues. With wife and co-author Diana Lynn Gray, he has written *Home Inc.* and *The Complete Canadian Small Business Guide* (both published by McGraw-Hill Ryerson). He is also president of the National Home Business Institute, a new association for home-based concerns.

In *Home Inc.*, the Grays write: "In the comfort of your own home or apartment, you can take your entrepreneurial desires and creative ideas and test them with minimal financial resources and risks."

The Grays feel strongly that decisions like this can't be made overnight. In fact, starting a home-based business is a rather lengthy process. It should begin, they believe, as all career decisions do, with a good, clear-headed look at yourself.

From his Vancouver office-at-home, Doug Gray outlines a seven-step process that anyone can use to test his or her interest and commitment.

Step 1

"You need to determine who you are and what you are at this point in your life," Gray says. "You need to assess your skills, attributes and talents; your strengths and weaknesses; your personal and occupational goals."

Step 2

"Look for an occupational pursuit," he suggests. "Determine what areas you have a natural affinity for. What do you enjoy that you can make money at?"

This might be work that you currently do that could also be done from home. As Gray points out, lots of home-based businesses get started when an employer becomes a client.

> "You need to determine who you are and what you are at this point in your life."

Step 3

"Determine if there's a natural fit between Steps 1 and 2," Gray advises. If there isn't, you may be able to take training to develop the skills and knowledge base necessary.

Step 4

"Do your research," he says. "Read everything you can on the subject matter. Take courses or seminars. Get to know your competition; who they are, where they are, how they charge for their services, what their strengths and weaknesses are."

Step 5

Develop a business plan. "Sit down and put your thoughts on paper," suggests Gray. "Take a look at the equipment you need and the brochure or advertising required. Outline your potential client base. Clearly define exactly what you intend to do."

Step 6

"Slowly test the idea on a part-time basis," Gray says. "See if you like it, if it fits, if you can make money."

Give yourself a realistic length of time to test the venture, he adds — "at least six months."

Step 7

"If it works and you like it, decide whether this is a full-time job or something you will continue to do part-time."

"It is important to start on a small scale," the Grays write in *Home Inc.* "This enables to you test your concept ... try out new ideas, test the market, determine what works and what doesn't, and develop confidence, experience and expertise and 'street smarts.' It allows to you change your mind completely ... all without much financial loss."

It's been predicted that by the turn of the century, 40 per cent of North American workers will work from home. An estimated 3.5 million Canadian workers and another 34 million in the U.S. already generate at least some of their income from offices, workshops or studios in their homes.

The growth, precipitated on one hand by the individual's need for independence and control, and on the other by the corporation's need to downsize and to offload overhead cost, means home-based workers will become a significant sector of the workforce.

Over the last year, marketing consultant and researcher Linda Russell, herself a home-based business person, designed and conducted a survey of such workers in Canada. Her research was limited to "technologically based home-workers," she says.

Fifteen hundred people attending two large computer shows, one in Vancouver, the other in Toronto, completed Russell's questionnaire. The results of that survey gave Russell, and the National Home Business Institute, which commissioned it, current data on Canadian home workers, she says.

Some 37 per cent of them run businesses out of their homes full-time, Russell discovered. Another 34 per cent hold traditional jobs while working from home to generate additional income. "Moonlighters," she calls them.

About 9 per cent "telecommute," she says, some as employees of a single firm, others as contract workers for several companies. The remaining 20 per cent bring work home from their regular jobs.

Sixty per cent of them are university educated, the survey found. Fifty per cent define themselves as "consultants." The average age of a Canadian home-office worker is 38, and the average yearly income of households in which there is a home-based business is $77,000.

Career Monitor undertook an informal small survey of another sort, when a reader from Brossard, Quebec, wrote to request information on the subject of "home employment for Canadians." The response from readers was immediate. Anyone considering working out of home will find their suggestions valuable.

• For those interested in investigating direct mail marketing, Toronto consultant Donald Lunny has written *Selling By Mail Order And Independence.* This guide, again totally Canadian, outlines the realities, pitfalls and profits to be made in this type of home-based business. Lunny's book, appropriately enough, is sold only by mail order.

• Two home-based professionals, Allan Cohen and Chris Ballard, are publishing *Working From Home,* a monthly newsletter.

For more information, write to Working From Home, 5 Durham Crescent, Aurora, Ontario, L4G 2V3.

• A couple of readers wrote to warn of advertisements for "home employment schemes" or directories of "Canadian home employment opportunities." Almost all the companies listed in such directories are in the U.S., according to one reader who had sent $25 for one. "It's misleading to use the word 'Canadian.'"

• *Start And Run A Home-based Business* by Edna Sheedy (Self Counsel Press) has some Canadian information, although its overall slant is North American.

• The National Home Business Institute (NHBI) is an association for home-based workers. With NHBI membership you get monthly information and networking meetings, quarterly newsletters, insurance programs, discounts on some services and products, and access to like-minded independent business people offering a variety of products and services.

For more information, write to the National Home Business Institute, 615 Mount Pleasant Road, Suite 234, Toronto, Ontario, M4S 3C5, or 1070 West Broadway, Suite 310, Vancouver, British Columbia, V6H 1E7.

In many ways the growing interest in home-based businesses is a sign of the times. Technology is becoming more affordable and "user friendly." Commuting is becoming more expensive, more difficult and a greater hazard. Overheads in traditional urban centre offices are increasing. And now, traditional jobs are becoming ever harder to find.

Still, anyone considering setting up a business at home needs to proceed with caution. As with the development of any new business venture, advance research and comprehensive planning is essential.

Part-time workers need protection

As the job market continues to transform itself, it's not always easy to understand what's going on. At times, the numbers of unemployed edge downward, sending encouraging signals of economic improvement. Under close scrutiny, however, those numbers don't always live up to their promise. The impression that valuable new jobs are finally beginning to reappear is false.

Some jobs are always being created, true enough, but those jobs aren't necessarily traditional, solid, full-time jobs. In fact, we have steadily been losing full-time jobs, even as thousands of new jobs make their appearance — many of them part-time.

The number of part-time workers in Canada — those who work fewer than 30 hours a week — is already well over two million. Most of them either prefer to work part-time or have personal circumstances that demand it.

Still, more than half a million of this country's part-time workers would love to find a full-time job, but can't.

Tim is one of them. After months of job hunting, he has only one likely prospect — and that company isn't ready to make a decision just yet. "I need to keep my grey cells working," Tim says, to explain why he accepted a two-day-a-week job as a market researcher.

Though an unwilling participant, Tim is now part of what's known as the "contingent labor force." This ungainly term refers to people who work temporarily, part-time, on a contract or "leased" basis, or to those who are self-employed. Since the early '80s there has been, as one American report suggests, a "phenomenal growth" of this contingent labor pool.

The industry that supplies temporary workers to Canadian employers is a case in point. Over the past 10 years, it has grown by 35 to 50 per cent, says Manpower Temporary Services vice-president Maureen Quinn, who chairs a committee for the Federation of Temporary Help Services.

The impetus for change was the 1981-82 recession, according to Edward Harvey, a sociologist with the University of Toronto's Centre for Industrial Relations. The "depth and severity of that recession was a chastening experience for many employers," Harvey says. They found themselves "facing very changed economic circumstances with large fixed overhead in terms of workforce."

So the "downsizing" began. "Competitiveness" became the byword of the business world. "Lean-and-mean" became a business cliché. By maintaining a smaller number of "core" employees, and hiring contingent workers as needed, companies have been able "to ride the cyclical punches more effectively," Harvey says.

Contingent workers assure companies "flexibility," he says. They can be "taken up or abandoned, depending on the nature of changes in supply and demand."

The "taken up" part of this new corporate philosophy is great for people like Helen, a senior secretary who prefers temporary work because of her own need for flexibility.

The "abandoned" part, however — which Helen, and lots of others like her, are experiencing right now — isn't so great. "It's makes me realize how vulnerable I am," she says.

Vulnerability is a fact of life for contingent workers. Not only is the work insecure and subject to the vagaries of the economic climate, contingent workers generally don't receive benefits or ready access to pension plans.

People working at the upper end of the scale — self-employed professionals, for example, and senior contract workers — either bill their time to compensate, or receive pay in lieu of benefits. At the lower end of the spectrum, however, workers are not confident and well trained. They tend to fall into jobs that require little skill, the vast majority of them in the low-paying service sector.

> "Contingent workers can be taken up or abandoned, depending on changes in supply and demand."

Workers at the bottom rung of the job ladder are generally those least able to stand up for themselves. "Women, young people, recent immigrants, and old people are over-represented," Harvey says.

Prakash works in a warehouse part-time. Two months ago, his manager cut his hours. "It's better than being out of work," Prakash says. "But I'm looking for another job. If something else comes along, I'll take it."

This lack of loyalty, understandable though it may be, is the downside for employers who hire contingent workers. In this economic climate, it doesn't pose much of a problem. In the future, however, it might.

Prakash, Tim, Helen and other contingent workers are on the losing side of the supply-and-demand tug-of-war at the moment. But later this decade, we're told, the supply of workers will start to shrink and demand will increase.

The business pressures that caused the growth in the contingent labor force haven't gone away. In fact, they have increased.

More and more workers, many of them disadvantaged, will fall into this category. By the turn of the century, 85 per cent of new entrants into the labor force will be women, new immigrants and people with disabilities, Harvey says.

Their rights need to be protected. Already there are rumblings among some part-time workers about the need to organize. Now would be the prudent time for employers and governments to begin framing enlightened public policy.

Chapter 13

LEARNING
TO KNOW
YOURSELF

ALFRED WONG

G etting to know yourself and making plans for the future are highly personal endeavors. Some people move along this path in order to build confidence. Others want to understand their skills and abilities so they can consciously manage them and build a satisfying career.

There's no single best way to begin self-assessment or personal development. Perhaps you can get what you need from books. Or maybe you have a friend, a mate, or a colleague who's willing to help, and good at drawing you out. Then again, you may prefer to pay a counsellor, or take vocational testing.

Whichever method works for you is the best one. In the end, you will probably use a combination of all of them. Techniques suggested in this chapter can get you started. For other publications, check the recommended reading list at the end of this book.

First you need an "I'm okay attitude"

Outwardly, Paula seems cheerful and in control. Behind that calm demeanor, however, her past and her future are locked in battle.

"I read the want ads every day. But I don't know. Everything seems beyond me — even the few that come up that sound like the job I used to do. I read them and think, 'I couldn't do that.' It's like I've forgotten everything."

Paula, a middle manager with more than 20 years' experience, has been out of work for nearly a year. She hadn't been excelling in the job she lost, so being laid-off didn't come as a big surprise. Still, it was traumatic. The past year of unemployment has sapped what little confidence she had left.

"Lengthy unemployment can erode confidence," says outplacement consultant Sy Eber. "People lose sight of the fact that they have skills and that they use them well. They move into the job market unsure of their skills."

This puts them at risk. "Employers pick up those vibes and turn off quickly," says Eber, an industrial sociologist. Employers are far more receptive, he says, to people who have what he calls, an "I'm okay attitude."

A positive attitude and personal confidence are founded on an understanding of one's own skills and abilities. These are the underlying requirements of a successful job-search campaign.

Skills, according to Richard Bolles in *What Color Is Your Parachute?* (Ten Speed Press) are "your God-given talents, gifts, aptitudes. They are the essence," he writes, "of what you have to contribute to the world, within the world of work."

Most everyone has 500 or so skills to his or her credit, says Bolles, who classifies skills into three broad categories.

• Specific work content skills, or technical skills, are peculiar to every job and generally not transferable to other jobs.

• Self-management skills, also known as interpersonal skills, relate to how we manage ourselves at work and in our personal lives. These skills, described by such words as enthusiasm, initiative, consistency, discipline, co-operativeness, judgment, reliability, sensitivity, stability, honesty, flexibility, resourcefulness and perseverance, are transferable to any activity or endeavor.

• So are functional, or motivating, skills, which relate to how we deal with information, people or things. Some motivating skills come so naturally to us, we often don't recognize them as skills. Some examples: analyzing/assessing, logical thinking, communicating, negotiating, managing, conceptualizing, supervising, teaching, counselling, persuading, planning, organizing, evaluating, administering and problem solving.

To begin assessing your own skills, Eber suggests you "ask people in the same job classification to talk to you. Get them to articulate what they do. Get titles for the work you did."

As well, Eber says, assess what the measures of performance were in your job.

In a recent New York Times article, businessman and professor Charles Handy suggests that you be-gin self-assessment by talking to peo-

> Some motivating skills come so naturally to us, we often don't recognize them as skills.

ple you know and simply asking them what you're good at. This direct approach can help you free up your thinking, he says. "Go to 20 people you know and ask each one to tell you one thing you do very well."

Career consultant Sandy Wise says you'll find evidence of your skills in the activities you enjoy — in your work and personal life. "If you're a student and you like talking to your friends and that's what you do for most of the day, obviously you have skills around communicating, and listening, around solving problems, and giving ideas," Wise says. "If you're into fitness, well, that takes perseverance, and discipline, and co-ordination."

Close scrutiny of just what you do on the job can also help indicate skills beyond your obvious technical skills, Wise suggests. "Take the salesman who says: `Well, I sell things. I tell people about the product and what it does.'

"That takes in the actual sales skill, but it also takes in the transfer-able skills — those subconscious things that he automatically moves into in order to do his work," Wise says. "A salesman has to be flexible, has to read his audience, make judgments and prepare his language to suit that audience."

Another way to begin examining skills is to assess, in detail, your accomplishments, and the contributions you've made over the years.

Yet lots of people, Paula among them, have trouble putting together a list of accomplishments because they really don't believe they have any.

If you're in this quandary, you'll need some help. Seek out people in your life who make you feel better about yourself. Tell them you need a little momentum and would benefit from talking to them for a while. Ask them to help you develop a list of your accomplishments. Ask them to interview you about the work you've done, as well as any other activities that you enjoyed. You might want to tape these interviews, so you can go back to them again and again in search of information about your skills and abilities.

Understanding the breadth and width of your own "skill set" is key to building and then maintaining a positive working life. This has never been more true than it is today. In a rapidly changing workplace, your natural aptitudes and the skills you acquire are the basis of your employability.

An understanding of your natural, transferable skills and a commit-ment to developing and upgrading the technical skills that complement them will go a long way toward ensuring your career security.

Follow your dreams

A period of restructuring and upheaval is not the best time to be changing your line of work. Still, there's no moratorium on thinking about it. In fact, job and career dissatisfaction often increases during uncertain times. Leaving a job in a tough business climate isn't wise, although if you're feeling dissatisfied, this is as good a time as any to examine the cause. Coming up with a long-term plan of action can at least give you a sense of control over your future.

Career change is often "tough for people to come to grips with," says ex-advertising executive, now career consultant, Jim Hayhurst, "be-cause they know there's going to be some pain in it. They're not quite sure how to get at it. And, there's no guarantee at the end that it's going to be better."

So people generally poke warily at thoughts of career change until something catapults them into it. At times it's a crisis, like getting fired or a marriage break-up, Hayhurst says. In other cases, people simply hit a brick wall. "They finally wake up one morning and say, `I'm not sure I can do this job one more day.'" And, sometimes, an "outside influence makes them stop and think about whether they're on the right mountain," he adds.

Hayhurst's own process of career change began when he sold Hayhurst Advertising. After 20 years in the ad business and precluded by his contract of sale from going back into it, he began to cast about looking for a new direction.

Not everyone has the luxury of spending a year and a half deciding what to do with the rest of his life. Hayhurst did. Like the advertising and marketing man he is, he had to discover the true essence of his product before knowing how to position it.

This time, his product was him.

He recalls emerging from that time with a strong sense that he was at his best when "helping people achieve their dreams."

> "You're successful if you're motivated. You're motivated if you're doing things that give you satisfaction."

Before tackling that goal, however, just as with any advertising campaign, Hayhurst had to do some research.

He spent a lot of time talking to senior executives, "looking for the ingredients of success," he explains. "I concluded that you're successful if you're motivated. And you're motivated if you're doing things that give you satisfaction.

"Then I tried to sit down and figure out what satisfaction was," he says. "I began to realize that satisfaction occurs when you're using your skills, in an area that interests you, with (others who have) a value system like yours."

Skills, interests and values — the cornerstones of career planning. Hayhurst is of the school that believes you can learn to understand them by carefully examining your past accomplishments and achievements. Intensive self-assessment is key, he says.

"Where you've been is a good indicator of where you're going," he says. A close look at your past can help build your future.

"Go back and look at activities in your life that gave you a real sense of satisfaction. Look at your education, your work experience, your extracurricular involvement, volunteer and personal activities.

"Look for things that *you* felt good about," advises Hayhurst. "Not your parents, not your peers, not society. They can be tiny little things. Anything that you did and walked away from feeling good about yourself."

Once isolated, break each incident down to find the skills, interests and values that are part of it, Hayhurst says. "It's a little like peeling an onion."

Don't stop the process until you find the thing that truly satisfies you. "You have to be honest and peel off each layer," he says. "You're looking for words that keep appearing again and again. These are your core skills, your core value system; the essence of you."

This exercise, while valuable, can be extremely difficult to do on your own. Objectivity is essential. You have to probe each incident relentlessly to find its core. You may need help. If you do, look for a friend who is good at saying 'why?' or 'explain that further,' says Hayhurst. "Look for someone who is prepared to be tough."

Once you begin to recognize your core values, skills and interests, "lay them on top of the job you're doing right now and find out what is causing dissatisfaction," Hayhurst advises.

"Then you can say, `Okay, I'm going to get out of this job and I know what kind of things to look for.' Or you can modify your own job."

In fact, he says, modifying your existing job may be preferable to changing it.

Hayhurst tells of a lawyer in mid-career who came to discover that it wasn't the practice of law that was making his life miserable but the responsibilities and headaches that went with being managing partner. He went to his partners and told them he wanted to give up his management role. Now, he's back doing what he loves best — working with clients on wills and estates.

Examine your values

The belief that job satisfaction is achievable, and maybe even a right, is a relatively new phenomenon.

Throughout much of our history, work was considered a means to an end. It was what one did to survive, to feed, clothe and take care of one's family.

With modern industrialization came a new awareness of work and our relation to it. The quest for job satisfaction began in earnest in the early '50s, in the Western world, at least. The service industry was emerging as a dominant force. Education became more accessible to more people.

As the post-war corporate world grew, the number of white-collar jobs expanded along with it. These jobs provided some degree of stimulation and challenge and workers began to seek them out. Increasingly, job satisfaction became a specific career goal.

The trend was given a significant boost in the early '80s, albeit in a rather back-handed way. During that recessionary period, many of the people who'd hitched their career wagons to large corporate horses suddenly found themselves cut loose. They were shocked. Loyalty to the corporation hadn't guaranteed their security as they'd assumed it would. There was a widespread sense of betrayal. People who'd long believed that mere employment was the basis of a happy existence began to question what they valued beyond that.

Since the early '80s, we've witnessed a growing interest in career issues. Losing a job — or leaving one that's unsatisfying — isn't a pleasant experience. Yet it can provide an opportunity to stop, take stock and ask: "What is really important to me? What am I good at? What kind of employer would respect me?" Perhaps, the thinking goes, if I knew myself better, and if I had a better understanding of today's complex workplace, I'd have an easier time knowing how and where to look for and find satisfying work.

There's no one definition of job satisfaction. It means different things to different people. And it often means different things at different times of life.

But, essentially, job satisfaction exists, according to career consultant Sandy Wise, "when you're using skills that energize you and when there's no conflict in values between you and your employer."

Wise is part of the industry that's developed to help people wade through the complexity of their own natures in search of work that's "right" for them. "Career consulting," it's called.

Job satisfaction is not the sole reason people seek career counselling, however. In many instances, expediency is the motivating force. Lots of people continue to view work as a means to an end. But in today's job market, with its shifting demands, anyone hoping to manoeuvre successfully needs a clear understanding of his or her skills and values.

We've already looked closely at the question of skills. But what of values? What's important to you? What motivates you? What do you strive for?

Hard questions, all of them.

"You can't just say to people, `think about what you value,'" observes human resources management consultant Estella Cohen. "You have to give them the words."

Here are some of the words Cohen and Wise and others in career consulting use. Pick your way through them. Choose five that best reflect what you value in an employer:

- location
- size of organization
- hours of work
- pleasant surroundings
- opportunities to advance
- educational assistance
- money
- security (full-time work versus part-time)
- your supervisor's style of management
- responsibility to the environment
- respect for employees
- social interaction with co-workers
- prestige or status
- ethical behavior

Now consider what you value in the job itself. Again, choose five:

- autonomy
- freedom of expression
- recognition
- structure
- achievement
- variety
- advancement
- mobility
- to be learning
- leadership
- responsibility
- challenge
- to see work completed
- order
- to be part of a team
- to be helping others
- to be doing something worthwhile

Though difficult to do, examining what you value in a job can help you pinpoint what in your current job might be causing you dissatisfaction. And if you're looking for work, knowing what you value in a job can help you articulate exactly what you're after.

Any discussion of values has several dimensions. This has been a look at subjective, personal values. Employers have values as well, generally expressed in terms of an organization's "culture."

In the years ahead, as the labor force shrinks, employers will again find themselves in competition for workers, we're told. As that happens, the unwritten rules that govern the job market will continue to change. Personal values and corporate values will increasingly be in search of each other. Tomorrow's employers are likely to be as concerned as you are that your values are fulfilled.

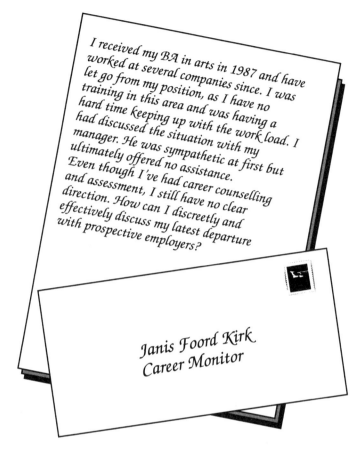

I received my BA in arts in 1987 and have worked at several companies since. I was let go from my position, as I have no training in this area and was having a hard time keeping up with the work load. I had discussed the situation with my manager. He was sympathetic at first but ultimately offered no assistance. Even though I've had career counselling and assessment, I still have no clear direction. How can I discreetly and effectively discuss my latest departure with prospective employers?

Janis Foord Kirk
Career Monitor

AND IN REPLY
The career counselling process isn't complete if you don't have a sense of direction. You've still got some career exploration to do. Go back to those you've already worked with or take your assessment to another counsellor and do what's necessary to find your preferred niche. Once you have, you'll be going on interviews for jobs that truly "fit." Then you can honestly discuss your last job as being a "poor fit."

Counsellors can help
identify your strengths

Nearly everyone finds it difficult to sift through his or her own nature in search of career insight. Some people — very few — can do it on their own with the help of a book or two and some general guidelines.

Most, however, need help.

"It's hard to be objective about yourself," one reader explained recently, adding: "I'm looking for some aptitude testing." Another reader wrote to ask: "Can you possibly refer some job or career services that might help me find a new position and new challenges?"

Aptitude, interest and personality testing can help when someone wrestling with the complexities of career change. But beware of the assumption that somewhere there is a test, or series of tests, or a counsellor that can tell you exactly what you should do with your working life. No such resource exists.

> ## "It's hard to be objective about yourself."

What testing *can* do is "increase your self-awareness," says registered psychologist and career consultant Scot McFadden. It can help you understand "what kind of boss you prefer," he says, "your life style preferences, your personality traits and what you value."

People with a broad range of interests often find testing helps them identify the ones that dominate, says McFadden. On the other hand, those with "undeveloped or very specialized interests" can be disappointed when looking for insight into new career areas, he says.

The number of career assessment services available to the general public is growing. This growth is expected to continue as workers at all levels — from the assembly line to the executive floor, attempt to learn how to manage their careers during troubled times.

When dealing with a career or vocational assessment service, expect to pay anywhere from $100 to $2,000. Often you can purchase a "package" of testing and counselling that begins with an initial meeting, followed by a series of tests. In a follow-up session or sessions you discuss what the testing indicates about you and your career options.

Should you prefer to work with an independent career consultant, you're wise to shop around. Ask friends and associates for referrals. As you research these services, assess not only the qualifications of the people with whom you'd work, but what Scot McFadden calls "your personal comfort level." Beware of counsellors who promise or guarantee that they can identify a career path that you'll enjoy, he adds.

Some consultants offer packages of testing and counselling, although you can also book time on a session basis. The cost per session usually runs in the $75 to $105 range. It often is possible for students or the unemployed to negotiate lower rates.

Before committing to any service or individual, get a clear sense of cost and what you can hope to achieve. Find out whether tests are used and if so, which ones. Ask about the counselling that's offered and the follow-up provided. Be definite. Ask probing questions.

Self-evaluation is just the first step in the career counselling process. Research and planning is next, then there's the actual job search. A concrete plan of action is the connecting thread that holds it all together.

Take time to determine your goals

For most of us, with the future so uncertain, with virtually every option dependent upon external forces largely out of our control, the thought of making progressive career plans seems next to impossible.

Nonetheless, goal setting is a worthy exercise.

Without realistic goals, too many people are inclined to spend the bad times waiting for good times to return; waiting for their old jobs to reappear and for life to get back to normal.

There's a growing sense, however, that what was "normal" in the job market of the late '80s is unlikely to be normal again.

Virtually every industry today is undergoing some form of restructuring. Many are shrinking, others are growing, few can avoid some sort of fundamental change. All kinds of jobs are vulnerable, and many people, even those working, are coming to the realization that nothing is guaranteed.

Setting goals can give you a sense of direction and control. Although difficult to predict, there's little doubt the future will be stressful, and high-tech. Machines will continue to revolutionize the way we do things. Economic problems, although they may moderate somewhat, are unlikely to disappear completely.

On a personal level, goals for the '90s will include gaining new skills. In business circles they will certainly include looking for new and creative ways to do business.

To begin protecting yourself, get informed about what's happening in your industry. Stay informed. Use this information to project and plan.

Even in shrinking industries, opportunities exist. The manufacturing sector, hit hard over the past few years, has lost about 20 per cent of its jobs. Yet, 80 per cent of manufacturing jobs still exist. And some new jobs are being created. Finding those healthy pockets, and acquiring the skills needed in them, is a valid goal.

When making plans for the future, take your whole life, not just your career, into account. More and more, people are looking for "balance" in their lives. Career goals, personal goals, social and even spiritual goals are unavoidably interwoven and all need to be considered when writing a personal strategic plan.

The uncertain state of the current job market makes this especially relevant. One unemployed woman put it this way: "I know what I want to do, but I have little hope of finding that kind of work right now. I'm into survival mode, and I'm looking for a survival job. I'll look for satisfaction in my private life."

> When making plans for the future, take your whole life, not just your career, into account.

Goal setting begins with the kind of self-assessment discussed throughout this chapter — and with a look at the lessons and mistakes of the past.

Find a quiet moment, sit down and write a short autobiography. Three or four paragraphs will do. Write about who you are and what you have done with your life. Close with a statement outlining where you are at the moment.

Next, make four separate lists. On one, list all the things you do well; on another, the things you don't do particularly well but for one reason or another must do. Next, note all the things you'd like to stop doing. And finally, make a list of the things you'd like to learn to do. Maybe it's time to take that computer course you've been putting off. Or to start the process toward accreditation in your field. (Increasingly, successful career management requires a commitment to what's called "life-long learning.")

Now, project into the future.

Pick a specific day, one year down the road; note it on the top of another sheet of paper — and let your fantasies float free. Imagine your life on that specific day — professional and personal:

- What are you doing?
- Where are you?
- Who are you with?
- How do you feel?

Note each thought in point form.

Then do the same thing again, for the same date a year later.

Once you have your fantasies down in back and white, let them sit for a few days. Then go back and take an objective look at what you've written.

From these few sheets of paper (or small computer file) you can develop a plan of action. Let the images you feel best about determine the steps you will have to take. What you're striving for is a written personal strategic plan that outlines:

- Where you are now
- The direction in which you're headed
- A longer-term objective (subject to change as you progress)
- How you're going to get there, and
- The obstacles you're likely to encounter along the way.

Say, for example, you've imagined yourself working in a different but related field. You'll have a lot of research to do. You'll want, as well, to discuss your plans with your family, then with people in your targeted field. If training is required, you'll need further research to find where the best training is available. You'll need to come up with the money, and the time, and the discipline to make it happen.

A word of caution.

When setting goals, strive to be realistic about what you hope to accomplish, and your timetable. Unrealistic goals can easily set you up for disappointment. At the same time, allow yourself to dream a bit. Be as clear as you can about those dreams. The motivation to achieve goals comes from an inner clarity.

The more confusing the times, the more valuable it is to have a clear personal sense of direction. Defining goals, even though you'll have to constantly up-date them, can alleviate some of the stress of the uncertain years ahead.

TIP

"The number one thing these days is to be focused, to know exactly what you want to pursue," says job search and networking specialist Colleen Clarke. "If you don't know exactly what you want to do, find out," she advises. "It's the hardest part of the process. It takes the longest. But once you're focused, the job search will be shortened."

Chapter 14

STARTING OUT

EMMANUEL LOPEZ

With planning, young people can improve job prospects

When there are more people looking for work than there are jobs, employers are less likely to hire young workers. It's pretty difficult to turn down all that specific experience out there in favor of untried talent.

"How can we compete?" several young people have written *Career Monitor* to ask. One, his frustration evident, added: "I wonder if experienced workers could always be found without giving people like us a chance?"

Today's statistics drive his point home. According to Statistics Canada, the unemployment rate for people between the ages of 15 and 24 is running almost double that for the work force as a whole. Being young, educated and raring to go in today's job market can be extremely frustrating.

Still, one's attitude makes a difference. Attitude helped one young graduate, Steve M., compete and win.

> "When I walked out with my degree, I felt stupid. I felt 'Everybody else has one of these things.'"

"To be honest, when I walked out with my degree, I felt stupid," Steve says, recalling a spring day in 1988 when he left university, an honors degree in economics tucked under his arm. "My parents were proud of me, but I felt, 'Everybody else has one of these things. It doesn't mean much.'"

Steve, who was just 24 at the time, soon found a degree did mean something. "It got my foot in the door," he acknowledges. "But experience got me interviews and won the job competition.

"There are so many ways to define experience," Steve says. His, for example, wasn't traditional work experience — but employers respected it nonetheless.

"In school, I was extremely active in extra-curricular activities," he says. "This ranged from student government, organizing sports, working at the newspaper and campus radio station." He also held down a part-time job, he says.

These endeavors were noted on his resume. "I never lied," Steve quickly points out. "I said this was strictly volunteer, but it gave me a lot of experience."

Too often, students do nothing throughout their university or college years but get a degree, he says. "Apathy is a problem on campus."

And it's this that puts them at a disadvantage when they enter the job market. "Get involved," Steve advises students. "Take advantage of the resources in your university or college. There's so much going on. Read the college newspaper and find out what's happening and attend some of these things.

"When you get involved, you can't help but have fun, and you get experience. It might not count now, but when you get into the job market, you're going to find that experience gives you a little edge. It will go a long way."

Steve's early experience, though part-time and volunteer, gave him an edge. In August 1988 he was offered a sales promotion co-ordinator's job with the Canadian branch of a major Japanese automotive company. He's since had a promotion and recently returned from a business trip to the corporate head office and plant in Japan. His career is very much on track.

According to the company's manager of human resources, Steve would have a good deal more competition if his resume landed on her desk today. Still, she says, she would interview him anyway. His extra-curricular activities spoke volumes about him, she adds.

"A lot of them related to sports and we're a recreational vehicle company," she explains. "It wasn't that he was out dirt bike riding. He was using his interest in sports in a business sense. He was writing press releases, doing communications, he was on the athletic council.

"He'd held the same part-time job for seven years," she adds. "Even though it was in a grocery store, it told me he was a good worker, and stable."

Steve found his way into the job market in happier times. It's impossible to say whether he'd have the same experience today.

But perhaps he would.

"We're a Japanese company, and very pro-hiring young people and training them," says the manager of human resources. "I like to keep a mixture of experienced people and university grads starting out."

More and more employers are following the lead of companies like this one and beginning to accept that even in a major downturn, it's essential to keep one eye on future needs. Nonetheless, competition for entry-level jobs is stiff, and it will continue to be for some time. Anyone looking for a first break should find a valuable lesson in Steve M.'s tale.

Last May, I graduated from a Radio and TV arts program. My goal is to become a studio camera operator for a large TV station. With my education and experience (cable TV) I thought I stood a good chance. I've sent out resumes, made phone calls and kept in touch with my school. So far, nothing has panned out. How can I grab someone's attention so they'll want to respond?

Janis Foord Kirk
Career Monitor

AND IN REPLY

If you're truly committed to this line of work, you're going to have to get more aggressive. You're trying to penetrate a tough industry, one already suffering from budget constraints.

Approach your cable TV contacts. Do they have work for you? Can they provide introductions to people working at the various TV stations? Ultimately, the person you want to meet is the technical director at each station.

Don't write this person. Call, say you're going to be in the vicinity and would like to drop in. Approach it casually, but try to discuss your training and your goals.

Be willing to start at the bottom. It's unlikely this will be a camera operator's job, by the way. Would you start as a cable puller just to get in the door? If so, be sure to make that clear.

You might be wise, as well, to try this same technique at stations in some of the smaller centres. Perhaps it will be easier to get experience there and move back into the large urban market in a year or two.

Teaching students to find work

At a moment's notice, most of us can tick off the summer and part-time jobs we held while in school. Perhaps we remember this early work with such clarity because it represented so many "firsts" — our first taste of independence, the first money that was truly ours, our first exposure to life outside our circle of family and friends.

Every year, hundreds of thousands of students head into the summer job market. The obvious goal is money, in many cases money to fund the coming year of study. Summer work provides more than that, however.

It's a testing ground. It's where young workers get experience, and references. Where they begin to develop work habits and learn what's expected of them in the work place. And sometimes, it's where students examine their career choices.

For more than 20 years, Canada Employment Centres for Students have been a conduit between employers looking for summer help and students looking for work. Each summer, hundreds of these centres across the country put students into about a quarter of a million jobs, says Delia DiNardo, who is district co-ordinator of 14 centres in the greater Toronto area.

When unemployment is high, the number of summer jobs that will be created is less certain.

To compensate, DiNardo says, the student employment centres have been putting a special emphasis on job-search workshops. Training in resume preparation and interview techniques will give young people some of the skills needed to gain a job-hunting edge.

Any young person in school — whether high school, college or university — who plans to return in the fall can use a student employment centre. Employers register summer jobs at their local centres. There is no direct charge to anyone using these centres.

The concept is quite clever — students helping students. Each centre is staffed by university students and supervised by a recent graduate. DiNardo, now a district co-ordinator, supervised a centre after graduating from university. Several years before that she got a summer job through a centre while going to high school.

"Because the centres are staffed by their peers, students feel at ease when they come in," DiNardo says. "It's hard to admit you don't know what to do in an interview, for instance. When you're talking to someone your own age, well, it's more comfortable."

People are approachable and the centres are "laid back," DiNardo says. Still, "there's lots of energy. People are very enthusiastic. People want to help."

Although job placement is the main focus of these centres, it's only one of the services provided.

"A student doesn't have to be looking for a job through us to use our service," says Doug McTaggart, another supervisor. "Some people may have job leads of their own and be pursuing them on an individual basis. They may just need some help writing a resume or getting ready for interviews, and we can help them do that."

There are many programs around — federal and provincial — to help young people start thinking about the direction of their working lives while they're still in high school and get some experience in fields of interest to them. But it's difficult for inexperienced people who don't understand the system to get at them.

As repositories for information of this kind, the centres offer young people another valuable resource.

"We're in the front line. We can refer people to government programs."

"We're on the front line," acknowledges Doug McTaggart. "We can refer people to government programs." Referrals can even be for next summer's job rather than this one. "A lot of the programs have deadlines," McTaggart says, "so it's important to apply early."

Canada Employment Centres for Students are open from May to August. Here's an outline of a few of their offerings:

SEED — Summer Employment/Experience Development

This program gives employers in the private and public sectors a wage subsidy to hire students. New jobs must be created and priority is given to jobs that relate, in some way, to the social priorities of the federal government — literacy, AIDS education, the environment, substance abuse and urban crime.

WOW — Work Orientation Workshops

Each year about 100,000 high school students leave school without graduating. This summer program is for those at risk of dropping out and those who already have. A mix of general life-skills training and work experience, it's designed to give young people a taste of life outside the school system, living on minimum wage.

Student business loans

Budding entrepreneurs with a summer business idea can get a loan of up to $3,000, repayable in October.

There are other programs — one for native students, for instance, and another one for university students who want to work in the federal civil service during the summer. There's also a host of provincial student programs.

Besides helping students find work this summer, Canada Employment Centres for Students will teach young people how to go about looking for work. They will use this skill time and time again as their careers develop.

*   *   *

Starting out in a new workplace is not solely a youth issue. New Canadians, many of them with years of experience and education to their credit, also have to work hard to break into our job market. The letter on the next page illustrates the difficulties and frustrations they face.

I am new to Canada and looking for work. Because I don't have "Canadian experience" I am not having much luck. I've asked different people just what this means and no one can tell me.

Janis Foord Kirk
Career Monitor

AND IN REPLY

Often, it means very little. It's simply an excuse some employers give to get you to go away. There are times, though, when it means that you don't yet understand how the Canadian system works and that familiarity is necessary to do the job in question.

I asked Bob Santos, an employment counsellor who often works with new Canadians, how one can combat the "no Canadian experience" objection when looking for work.

Be prepared to highlight your transferable skills, Santos advises. "Universal things, like honesty, dependability, dedication to a task, an ability to grasp new concepts, to learn quickly, willingness — everyday things that everybody in the world deals with."

If you have post-secondary education, have it evaluated. Check with a major university to find out how to do that.

If there's a job you particularly like and feel you could do, you could tell the employer that you're willing to offer your time, on a voluntary basis for a couple of weeks. In that way, the employer can assess your abilities on the job, Santos says.

Chapter 15

DAY-TO-DAY ON THE JOB

Performance appraisal can work for you

How well do you perform on the job? How clearly, accurately and objectively is that performance assessed? And is your present performance adequate to guarantee your future earning potential?

No one, on either side of the employer's desk, looks forward to performance reviews with much enthusiasm. Nowadays, they're even more difficult. Managers are under tremendous pressure to cap costs and, at the same time, increase worker productivity. Workers, on the other hand, are feeling vulnerable, and often don't know where to turn for help and advice.

One of them, Bob, writes: "What do you do in a situation where you feel you're being overworked and not paid fairly?"

In his company, Bob goes on to say, December is performance appraisal time. He feels his performance has been rated low so the company can "justify a low salary increase."

> "What do you do when you feel you're being overworked and not paid fairly?"

Still, Bob likes his job, the people and the work environment. His employer recently discussed the possibility of improved benefits and training opportunities. Bob feels, however, that this is only a "ploy to comfort employees who are about to get a lousy raise."

Should he tell his employer that he's not pleased and will be looking for new work? he asks. Or should he simply be thankful to have a job as "the economy is in such poor shape?"

Tough questions, these, and virtually impossible to answer without more information. What sort of shape is his company in? for example. What's the going rate for jobs like Bob's in his industry? How likely is he to replace it at a higher salary? How finely tuned are his job-search skills?

Nonetheless, Bob's quandary brings into sharp focus a broader concern worth examining against the changing backdrop of the workplace of the '90s.

If we're going to compete and thrive in our complex world economy, we're going to have to change the way we do things, and, for that matter, the way we think.

Performance appraisals, for example. Traditionally, worker assessment of this sort has "looked backward rather than forward," says Don Hathaway, partner in charge of human resources at Ernst and Young. "It's been a way of reviewing what an employee has accomplished and looking at areas that need improvement." Largely, it's been an administrative function, he adds, that creates a record for the employee's file on which to base compensation, or training decisions, or remedial action.

Although "depressingly slow," there's a dawning awareness that performance appraisals of this kind are limited, and limiting, Hathaway says — and that a golden opportunity is being missed.

Rather than appraising performance, supervisors in the future will have to manage it, he says. And in so doing, they will help their staff manage their careers.

To date, only a few, progressive companies have adopted this "more proactive approach," Hathaway says. In such companies, "there is consultation between employers and employees. Together they lay out a plan for what the employee is going to do on behalf of the company, what developmental needs will be addressed. There's an ongoing review throughout the year."

Such organizations are also looking for ways to make vague performance requirements more concrete, says Mark Jackson, a senior principal with Hay Management Consultants. "Not just saying we want you to display more initiative, but actually isolating what initiative looks like." Over time, this will make the performance management system,"more transparent,"he says, and, ultimately, more equitable.

What might this mean to Bob, and others like him trying to build positive careers in these complicated times?

In the short term, very little probably — although both Jackson and Hathaway suggest that Bob re-examine his view of what his employer is offering. Business is not exactly booming, and the amount being offered "is not a bad increase," says Jackson. And, he points out, training and improved benefits are two "creative ways for employers to encourage innovation and pay people for their contributions. Training increases an employee's capabilities," he explains. "And it says, `we're investing in you.'"

According to Hathaway, employees in general need to examine their thinking. "There's a mentality out there that says ' big business is bad and I should get everything I can,'" he says. "It also says, 'if I do a great job, I should get more money.'"

Already, Canadian salaries are too high, Hathaway says. As a workforce needing to compete with other workforces around the world, we have to give up our expectation of yearly increases beyond the cost of living. "If you do a great job, your reward is that you get to keep the job," he says. "You get more money when you take on more responsibility, or get a promotion."

Employers, too, need to look closely at the way they do things, he adds. Most don't communicate well, for example. "They don't take time to explain what's important to them, why they do what they do," Hathaway says. And they often don't train managers well — one of the main reasons performance appraisal meetings are so poorly handled as a rule.

"On Friday afternoon, we take the best engineer or the best sales rep and promote them," Hathaway says. "By Monday morning, we expect them to know about space allocation, about renting computers, departmental budgets and about managing people.

"We expect managers to judge performance and then tell their staff about it, for example. But we never train them to do it."

As times change, so do the rules. Performance, training and advancement are now bound together. Employers need to accept that performance management is incomplete without a training component. For their part, employees have to come to view training as a valuable asset in their own career development.

So you're stuck with a bad boss

"My career was in pretty good shape until George came on the scene," recalls Malcolm L. "He was picky and demanding. He said one thing and did another. He undermined my authority all the time...."

Few things can make your life miserable like working for a difficult boss. It's disheartening, and demoralizing, and it can throw your career into a tailspin.

Malcolm is an engineer by trade. For most of his career — nearly 20 years — he has worked for the same resource company. For 10 of those years, he was a project manager. Then he moved into marketing, where he found his niche, he says. He progressed with seeming ease into middle management.

During the merger mania of the '80s, the firm Malcolm worked for was bought by another company. For a time, he thought he'd be a casualty of the merger. He wouldn't have minded much, he says. "Morale was incredibly low. Everyone was looking over their shoulder."

He survived the crunch — sort of. Blending two different corporate cultures can create casualties of another kind. The marketing department got a new senior manager with an autocratic management style.

Malcolm and his associates, used to a high degree of autonomy in their work, found themselves playing in an entirely new ball park under a new set of rules.

A family man who values stability and security, Malcolm put a lot of effort into making the new situation work. "I knew I wasn't handling things very well," he admits. "But I could never find the right approach. I don't know anybody like this guy. And I don't respect him much."

The months progressed and Malcolm, normally taciturn by nature, became more and more withdrawn, his wife says. He lost confidence in himself. He stopped spending as much time with his children. Occasionally, he suffered from vague and undefined symptoms of illness. And for the first time ever, he called in sick a few mornings when he really could have gone to work.

Feeling trapped in an untenable work situation can be extremely frustrating. Loyalty and his own need for security bound Malcolm for several years to a job that no longer satisfied, working for a man he didn't respect.

Others, in similarly unhappy work relationships, say lucrative salaries, or our tight job market, or the fear that there's nothing else they can do, trap them.

Two American psychologists, Mardy Grothe and Peter Wylie, have written a book for people caught in this dilemma called *Problem Bosses, Who They Are And How To Deal With Them* (Fawcett Crest). Early in the book, the authors attempt to explain why some bosses are so impossible.

> "I knew I wasn't handling things very well, but I could never find the right approach."

Being a boss is a tough job, they write. At the same time, bosses are just ordinary people. They don't have strong role models and they often aren't trained well.

And they don't become bosses because of their ability to manage people.

Bosses often can't handle power and authority, the authors say. They don't necessarily have to answer to anyone else themselves. And in a large number of cases, they seldom bother to solicit feedback from their employees.

The book offers about a dozen strategies for dealing with problem bosses, outlining the pros and cons of each.

The most common response, the authors say, is to "do nothing." Or, at least, to seem to do nothing. The appearance of inaction is deceptive, however, because "nothing" is not really a response within the capabilities of most people.

Unexpressed anger festers. People complain, vent their frustration to others. Or, as Malcolm L. did, they internalize their anxiety. Still others slack off, or escape into alcohol or drugs.

A far better strategy, the authors suggest, is to decide to accept your boss as he or she is, to become more tolerant of what they call "different operating styles." Or, to work to change yourself, to change your own thoughts and feelings, and in so doing, gain the upper hand.

"It never occurred to me there might be ways to take control of the situation," says Malcolm.

A good approach, the authors say, is to apply the principle of "managing up." Devote some time and energy to getting to know what makes your boss tick. There are ways to meet many of his or her wants and needs (and in so doing, get your boss on side) without compromising your own integrity, they maintain.

> Devote some time and energy to getting to know what makes your boss tick.

A more direct approach is to request a meeting with your boss on your own, or in a group, to discuss the problem. This strategy requires a lot of planning and will work with some bosses and not others, Grothe and Wylie caution.

A less direct, but relatively low-risk way to get your point across is to send an anonymous letter or note, they say. One example given in the book is that of the employees who sent flowers to their boss's wife with a condolence card that read: "We only have to work with him. You have to live with him."

The book also looks at several high-risk strategies. You can go over your boss's head. Or, you can take a stand and file a grievance, take legal action, or become what's called a whistle-blower. These are obviously not for the faint of heart, however.

Wylie and Grothe also examine an option they call "firing your boss." Leaving a boss — and a job — is a specific career development step, they point out. It should be approached as such and carefully planned.

Malcolm eventually adopted that suggestion. He got around his problem boss by transferring to a new boss. Though it wasn't a great career move, he feels better about himself these days. "I do miss the marketing environment," he admits. "But I don't miss the aggravation."

In a telephone interview from his office in Boston, Grothe answered the following questions from people struggling to find ways to deal with their own problem bosses:

How do I get recognition in a company where my boss takes credit for everything I do? He never allows his staff exposure to senior executives.

Credit-takers are among the most common problem bosses, Grothe says. "It's inherent in the role that has power and authority. It's annoying to employees and a huge source of resentment.

"Some credit-taking bosses are good people," Grothe observes. In fact, he says, "there is a certain amount of credit-taking potential in all of us. It's quite common for people to enhance their own contribution."

If your boss is approachable, ask for a "direct, one-on-one, sit-down session," Grothe advises. "He may just need to be reminded of what's important. State clearly that when credit is taken for the work you do, it makes you feel deflated, de-motivated and, to be honest, a little resentful."

Ask that your boss let senior management know how hard you and others work on projects. Point out that, once that happens, "you'll all appreciate him more and work much harder for him in the future," Grothe says.

This strategy won't be very effective with "bosses who have a selfish and neurotic need for recognition, or who are so insecure that they become defensive and vindictive at the slightest criticism," he adds.

They require a different approach.

"If you're afraid that once the report you've finished gets on your boss's desk he or she will take all the credit, send copies of the first draft to several other people (including your boss's boss) with an appropriately dated memo, asking for feedback and helpful suggestions," Grothe advises.

How do I handle a boss who is combative, stubborn, aggressive and really abusive in one-on-one situations, and Mr. Nice Guy in front of senior management?

"Ask your boss to discontinue this practice," Grothe says. Tell him that when he talks to you in that manner, "it hurts you and de-motivates you. Do that once, maybe twice. If it doesn't stop, get out of the relationship. People who stay in abusive relationships pay a heavy emotional price," he says. "Their self-confidence erodes. They begin to experience feelings of depression and anxiety. If it's clear that it's not going to change, get out."

How can I deal with a boss who asks me to hide things from senior management? It goes against my ethics to do this.

People in this situation have three alternatives, Grothe says. They can go along with the situation and risk all the guilt and fear and apprehension that go with it. They can "exit the scene." Or they can find a way to expose the situation.

Going over your boss's head is a risky move, Grothe says. You might be wise, instead, to adopt what he calls "the indirect approach." Look around in your organization for an individual, either a peer or superior to your boss, who is concerned with equity and fairness and justice. Approach this person, saying you need someone to confide in. It is to be hoped that he or she will be willing to act as a mentor, or possibly even intervene on your behalf.

> "It could be that your boss is insensitive and doesn't see things from your perspective."

How do I handle a new boss who undermines my position? He has taken over some of my responsibilities, he calls up my clients and takes them to lunch. I learn about this in memos.

You need to decide whether your boss is a devious person or you are misinterpreting his motives, Grothe says.

"Talk to him," he suggests. "Tell him that you're puzzled by these actions. Ask why they are happening. Ask to be kept informed.

"It could be that your boss is insensitive and doesn't see things from your perspective, and this will be a helpful reminder that his actions are being misinterpreted. If so, he'll change.

"If he's a devious type, he's going to say `certainly' and do nothing. How he responds will determine what you eventually do."

In the final analysis, "Your choice of a particular strategy is going to be determined by the kind of person you are," Grothe says, "your values, your personality, your situation in life, even your age.

"Young people are likely to take some of the riskier strategies. If you're 46, paying a hefty mortgage and educating a couple of kids, you'll gravitate to the more conservative solution," he says.

"Before taking any action, identify what you are comfortable with."

I have worked in the same corporation for more than five years. I consider myself to be professional in both manner and dress, and believe I'm regarded in the the same way by colleagues.

Here's the problem. Some people are calling me by names of endearment. I'm not talking about the kindly older woman who calls everyone "dear" regardless of sex, age or position. I don't take offence to that.

The people to whom I refer are (with) the companies providing services to my corporation; we are their client, and I am their liaison.

Can you provide some suggestions on how to correct the people who call me "hon" and "love" and "sweetie"?

Janis Foord Kirk
Career Monitor

AND IN REPLY

Questions of etiquette, business and otherwise, are answered regularly in the Toronto Star's Life Section by Ms Manners, a.k.a. Judith Martin. I tracked her down and put your question to her.

Ms Manners believes that endearments are not suitable for office use. She suggests that you correct these people, taking care to do it gently. The next time you're addressed in this manner, say, pleasantly, "My name is not Hon, it's ...."

Persist, and you'll soon get your message across.

Head hunters on the prowl

It's 10:10 a.m. You're at your desk, in the middle of what's cooking up to be a busy morning. The phone rings. You answer, expecting to hear a familiar voice asking one of the many questions that punctuate your days.

Instead, an unfamiliar voice addresses you by name and says:

"You were referred to me. I'm looking for an operations manager for a busy and growing communications firm. You would report directly to the president and be responsible for managing about 25 people. You'd get involved in every part of the organization. You'd have a lot of freedom. The pay is in the $65,000 range. Are you interested or do you know of anyone who might be?"

You've just been approached by a head hunter. Or, possibly, by a researcher working on a head hunter's behalf. If this is the first time you've received a call like this, you're probably stuck for words. You might also be a little suspicious.

At the same time, even if you love your job, you're tantalized.

> "At one point, people were very suspicious. Now, they want to hear what you have to say. It's an ego trip to be recruited."

"Most people are complimented," says Peter Shenfield, who could be one of the people on the other end of the line. Shenfield, a partner with E. L. Shore and Associates Corp., has been a head hunter for more than 20 years. Today, people are more receptive to his calls than they once were, he says.

"At one point, people were very suspicious. They wouldn't talk. Now they want to hear what you have to say. It's an ego trip to be recruited."

Jack Harris, of the executive recruiting firm Gerry Baker And Associates, agrees. Head hunting calls, once used mostly to recruit senior executives, now "work at just about any level," Harris says. "There's an increasing awareness and acceptance of them. Because of today's business climate, more and more people are at least receptive to hearing about opportunities."

Many of the opportunities head hunters call to discuss are never advertised — which isn't to say that recruiting firms, as a rule, don't advertise. Some advertise extensively and are well known because of it. Anyone who reads the career section of a large newspaper regularly will know of them.

Still, there are recruiting firms, Shenfield's and Harris' among them, that seldom advertise. They prefer to operate behind the scenes, using what Shenfield calls the "direct recruiting" approach.

"It's far more efficient," Harris says. "You can target specific organizations or individuals, rather than waiting for the right resume to come through the door."

The targeting process that Harris describes begins long before the call that interrupts your busy morning. As a first step, the recruiter, the employer, and sometimes a researcher, get together and flesh out the criteria for the job. Next, a head hunting strategy is developed.

In some instances, once the strategy is in place, the recruiter works the front lines. He or she deals with the client and, once a short list is together, conducts one-on-one interviews with job applicants. The researchers—whether on staff or on contract—work behind the scenes and do most of the digging. In other instances, though, the recruiter handles the entire assignment.

However it's handled, research is a big part of the process. "We use directories, data bases, library research, and resumes we have on file," says Shenfield. "We also rely on our knowledge of the industries in which our clients operate. We might approach suppliers, customers and other professionals in the field."

The object of this research is to develop of a list of people who, on paper at least, fit the job. As potential names come up, either the recruiter or the researcher will place a call.

"In the telephone contact, we try to develop a more complete understanding of the individual's academic background, work history, areas of specialization and compensation needs," says Harris. "We're also trying to find out if they're interested in looking at alternatives."

Not everyone is, he acknowledges. But "networking" is a secondary benefit to the head hunting call, Harris says. "The individual might say, `This job's not for me, but here's someone else you should talk to.'"

Shenfield says that 80 to 85 per cent of the people he approaches are willing to listen to what he has to say. From them he gets information and new leads and, eventually, people who fit his criteria. The individuals on the other end of the line get the chance to conduct a little job market research of their own with an "expert."

Keep in mind, not everyone who calls himself a head hunter will be an expert. As in most fields, some people are better qualified and more professional than others.

Should you receive a head hunting call, heed this advice from Jack Harris: "If a call is unprofessional, and information is not forthcoming, ask for a number, and do your own research into the head-hunting firm before giving information."

Chapter 16

MANAGING
THE
FUTURE

Sami Suomalainen

Training is the key

"**Y**ou don't have to tell me I need to learn how to do something else," said Marjorie, who had wedged herself into a corner of the small room. "But I don't know where to begin.

"I never even finished Grade 10," she continued, her voice shaking. "I've been working out there for nearly 20 years."

She jerked her thumb at the factory floor outside. "I thought I'd be there `til I retired."

Around the crowded room, heads nodded in agreement. "And I've still got a 16-year-old at home," she continued. "What am I supposed to do?"

Across the country, hundreds of thousands of workers have been asking questions like these. Some, like Marjorie and her co-workers, have been laid off. Their need is immediate, and urgent. But lots of other people, even those who are relatively secure in their jobs, are feeling vulnerable these days. They're questioning whether their skills are adequate to protect their livelihoods in the future. And frequently, they're not.

Training is a key issue for all of us as we try to make sense of the restructuring under way in our workplace.

So just whose responsibility is it to train, and when necessary re-train, Canadian workers? Whose job is it to see that the workforce has the skills needed to compete and thrive in the dog-eat-dog international marketplace?

It's a good question. And Canadians have yet to come up with a satisfactory answer.

As a society, our training policy has been shortsighted. In fact, we lag significantly behind all other industrialized nations when it comes to training programs already in existence.

Rich with natural resources, we have been able to get by with little attention to the future needs of our labor force.

Until now.

As technology continues to transform the very basis of production, job seekers often don't have the skills required to land the jobs available. With each passing year, the worrisome gap widens between the skills we have in our society, and the ones we need.

In the not-too-distant future, labor shortages threaten, particularly among technicians, professionals, managers, supervisors and skilled tradespeople.

And who are we counting on to come into the workplace and fill the void? Young people, women and minorities mostly.

A 1991 survey of employers conducted by the Hudson Institute and Towers Perrin, a human resources consulting firm, found that although corporate Canada is aware of these changes and their potential impact, little is being done to prepare for them. Many companies are "close to survival mode," explains Don Brooks, a consultant with Towers Perrin. "There's a lot of preoccupation — for valid reasons — with today, tomorrow or next year."

A great many workers are in survival mode as well, right now, preoccupied with the problems of the moment, rather than with long-term career goals. Nonetheless, says Brooks, the need for advanced training will increase: "About 50 per cent of jobs created in the next 10 years will require 17 years of education."

The demands of a new, competitive age are catching up with us. What's desperately needed if Canada is to meet the challenges of the next century is the development of a "training culture."

So says Laurent Thibault, co-chair of the National Labourforce Development Board.

"What we have to do is shift our thinking to the sources of growth and wealth in the future," Thibault says. "It's a mind-set that we have to have as a country. We have to believe more strongly in the fact that the real strength of our country is going to be in the skills and knowledge base of its labor force."

> "The real strength of our country is in the skills of its labor force."

In many parts of Canada, our standard of living, based as it is on commodities and natural resources, has reached its "physical limits," he says. Growth in the future will increasingly be based on "knowledge, technology, skills and information."

The role of the board, also known as the National Training Board, is to "bring together the major players," Thibault says, and to build a consensus among the partners in training — labor, management, education and the other training institutions.

It's a tall order. The major players have not always felt particularly co-operative. And bickering between the partners in the training process has marred, and often thwarted, training initiatives in the past.

That must change, says Thibault.

"The educational institutions themselves (must change), and the extent to which they are responsive to the needs of the marketplace;

business people (must change), to the extent that they can increase the priority they give and the commitment they make to improving skills of the labor force.

"The labor movement as well has its own dynamics," Thibault continues. "It has some distance to travel. We all do. We all look and see the shape our country is in economically. We're all getting a sense that we have to do things differently.

"It's a question of moving the country forward on a broad front."

The 22-member board will attempt to combine these factions in a working forum to "come up with a real consensus and strong recommendations," says Thibault. In the near future, he insists, you will find "a lot of activity and energy being directed to finding more imaginative solutions than in the past, where we simply sat in each other's camps and lobbed grenades over the fence."

Above and beyond this apparent ceasefire, the National Training Board will be looking for ways to effectively use the hundreds of millions of dollars diverted from the unemployment insurance fund into retraining programs.

Co-chair Gerard Docquier noted the "abominable lack" of counselling for laid-off workers. "We have to provide them counselling that will allow them to find their niche in the new labor market," he said.

So, can Marjorie and the millions of other Canadian workers rest easy, now that the National Training Board is on the case?

"I think you know the answer to that," says Thibault. "The challenge is there. The need is real. There's mounting evidence that we're not doing the job on training. But, we've got a lot of homework to do."

RECOMMENDED READING LIST

Do What You Love, The Money Will Follow
by Marsha Sinetar,
Dell Books.

Escaping The Pink Collar Ghetto
by Roberta Cava,
Key Porter Books.

Guerrilla Tactics In The Job Market
by Tom Jackson,
Bantam Books.

Home Inc.,
by Douglas A. Gray and Diana Lynn Gray,
McGraw-Hill Ryerson.

How To Get A Better Job In This Crazy World
by Robert Half,
Crown Publishers.

I Got Fired Too
by Jill Jukes and Ruthan Rosenberg,
Stoddart Press Inc.

Now It's Your Move
by Frederick W. DeRoche and Mary A. McDougall,
Prentice Hall.

100 Best Companies To Work For In Canada
by Eva Innes, Jim Lyon and Jim Harris,
Harper Collins.

Problem Bosses
by Mardy Grothe and Peter Wylie,
Fawcett Crest.

Psycho-Cybernetics
by Maxwell Maltz,
Simon and Schuster.

Re-Careering In Turbulent Times
by Ronald L. Krannich,
Impact Publications.

Selling By Mail Order And Independence
by Donald Lunny,
available only by mail order
from Productive Publications,
P.O. Box 7200, Station A, Toronto, Ontario, M5W 1X8.

Street Smart Selling: The Ultimate Guide To Masterful Persuasion
by Andrea Moses,
Powerbase Consultants.

The Career Directory
by Richard Yerema and Peter Angelou,
Edcore Publishing.

The Complete Canadian Small Business Guide
by Douglas A. Gray and Diana Lynn Gray,
McGraw-Hill Ryerson.

The Only Job Hunting Guide You'll Ever Need
by Kathryn and Ross Petras,
Poseidon Press.

The Right Place At The Right Time
by Robert Wegmann and Robert Chapman,
Ten Speed Press.

What Color Is Your Parachute?
by Richard Nelson Bolles,
Ten Speed Press.

Your Perfect Right— A Guide To Assertive Living
by Robert E. Alberti, PhD, and Michael L. Emmons, PhD,
Impact Publishers.

KIRKFOORD COMMUNICATIONS INC.

Kirkfoord Communications is a partnership dedicated to the furtherance of direct and honest communications. We offer a complete communications service based on shared values. Our specialties include social marketing, career development, innovative training videos, corporate communications and television production.

We believe that information is a valuable asset to be dispensed with integrity and candor.

For more information, write or fax:

Kirkfoord Communications Inc.
422 Cam Fella Boulevard
Stouffville, Ontario, Canada L4A 7G8

Fax: (416) 642-2656

INPRINT EDITORIAL SERVICES

Inprint is a partnership offering printed communications using computers for input, graphics and final output. We offer skills in editing writing, photography, layout and design and produce a fully paginated final result. We are dedicated to accuracy, reliability and performance.

For further information, write or fax:

Inprint Editorial Services
30 Church Street
Suite 604
Toronto, Ontario, Canada M5E 1S7

Fax: (416) 368-3776

You can order additional copies from:

Toronto Star Syndicate
P.O. Box 1700, Station R
Toronto, Ontario
M4G 4A3

Please send me _____copies of *Surviving The Upheaval In Your Workplace* by Janis Foord Kirk at $14.95 each (which includes postage, handling and applicables taxes).

I am enclosing a cheque or money order for _____

Please send by return mail to:

_____

_____

_____

_____

Discounts are available on orders of 10 books or more.
For more information, please write:

Kirkfoord Communications Inc.
422 Cam Fella Boulevard
Stouffville, Ontario
L4A 7G8

Or fax: (416) 642-2656